CU01464414

SENEGAL

TRAVEL GUIDE

Your Travel Companion To Wander, Explore, And Savor The Highlights Of This Must-Visit Destination

Lawrence P. Hardy

Copyright © 2025 Lawrence P. Hardy
All Rights Reserved.

PLEASE READ ME!

Thank you for choosing our travel guide. We are committed to providing comprehensive and reliable travel insights, ensuring that the information presented is as accurate as possible. However, travel conditions can change quickly and unexpectedly.

We recognize that travelers depend on our guide for trip planning and decision-making. While we strive for precision, details such as operating hours, pricing, and service availability may differ from what is listed. We strongly recommend verifying essential information, particularly for time-sensitive activities, reservations, or scheduled plans.

Your safety is our priority. We encourage you to stay aware of your surroundings, exercise standard travel precautions, and remain informed about local conditions. Each destination has its own unique characteristics and challenges, so it's important to follow current guidelines, respect local customs, and make choices based on your comfort level.

You may notice that some information appears in multiple sections of this guide. This is intentional, as most travelers refer to different topics as needed rather than reading straight through. For example, restaurant details may be found in both the dining section and must-visit listings, while safety guidelines may be included in general advice and specific neighborhood descriptions. **This strategic repetition minimizes the need for constant cross-referencing, ensuring you have the key details whenever and wherever you need them.**

Feel free to explore the guide in any order—each section is designed as a complete resource, allowing you to plan your journey smoothly without flipping between pages.

TRAVEL MAP

SCAN QR CODE FOR MAP & MEDIA

- Open your QR code scanner (download one from your app store if needed).
- Aim your camera at the QR code to scan it.
- Tap the link that appears after scanning to access the map.
- The link will direct you to the map of your travel destination.
- When prompted, allow the map to access your location for accurate navigation.
- On the map, click "Directions" to get detailed instructions to your destination.
- For the starting point, select "Your Location" (this may require granting location access to your device).

- For the destination, type in the specific location from this guide that you are heading to.

TO ACCESS MEDIA

Scroll down to see the "Photos" or "Videos" section after the map page has come up. With this, you will be able to see other tourists reviews and ratings who have previously visited the destinations and establishments.

TABLE OF CONTENTS

CHAPTER 1.

INTRODUCTION TO SENEGAL

Welcome to Senegal, a vibrant West African nation renowned for its rich cultural tapestry, stunning natural landscapes, and warm hospitality, famously known as "teranga." This guide is meticulously crafted to provide you with a comprehensive roadmap to navigating Senegal, from bustling urban centers like Dakar to serene natural retreats like the Casamance region.

Every section of this guide is designed to ensure your journey is immersive, enjoyable, and seamless. Whether you're planning your first trip or returning to explore deeper, this guide will enhance your understanding of Senegal and ensure you experience it like a seasoned traveler

Why Visit Senegal?

Senegal is more than just a country in West Africa—it's a vibrant tapestry of history, culture, natural beauty, and warm hospitality. Often called the "Gateway to Africa," Senegal is an extraordinary destination where travelers can immerse themselves in rich traditions, explore stunning landscapes, and enjoy unforgettable adventures.

Cultural Richness and Hospitality (Teranga)

Senegalese culture is deeply rooted in the philosophy of "Teranga," which translates to hospitality. This principle is not just a cultural trait but a way of life, where visitors are treated as family. Tourists will often find themselves warmly welcomed into homes, festivals, and ceremonies, creating lasting connections with locals.

- **Highlight**: Visit a traditional **village in the Casamance region** to experience local customs, taste authentic dishes, and learn about indigenous Diola traditions.

A Living History Lesson

Senegal's history is interwoven with colonialism, the transatlantic slave trade, and independence movements, making it a significant cultural and historical destination.

- **Gorée Island**: A UNESCO World Heritage Site, it is a poignant reminder of the transatlantic slave trade. The **Maison des Esclaves** (House of Slaves) offers a sobering look at this dark chapter in history.
- **Saint-Louis**: The colonial architecture in this former French capital of West Africa showcases the blending of African and European influences. Guided walking tours highlight the city's unique history.

Vibrant Arts and Music Scene

Senegal is a global cultural powerhouse, thanks to its dynamic arts and music traditions.

- **Music**: The birthplace of mbalax, a high-energy fusion of traditional drumming and modern instruments. Dakar hosts music festivals like the **Dakar Music Festival** in March.
- **Art**: Dakar's vibrant art galleries, such as the **Galerie Le Manège**, display works from contemporary African artists. The **Biennale de Dakar**, held every two years, is a must-visit for art enthusiasts.

Natural Wonders and Biodiversity

Senegal's geography offers something for every nature lover:

- **Lac Rose (Pink Lake)**: Known for its surreal pink hue caused by algae and high salinity. Travelers can take guided canoe tours or float in the buoyant waters.
- **Niokolo-Koba National Park**: A UNESCO-listed wildlife reserve where safari-goers can spot elephants, lions, and rare antelope species. Entrance fees start at 15,000 XOF per person.
- **Djoudj Bird Sanctuary**: A paradise for birdwatchers, this wetland reserve is home to over 400 bird species, including pelicans and flamingos.

Unparalleled Beaches and Water Adventures

Senegal's coastline stretches over 500 kilometers, offering pristine beaches and vibrant marine life.

- **Petite Côte**: Perfect for relaxation, with golden sands and tranquil waters. Popular spots include **Saly** and **Popenguine**.
- **N'gor Island**: A haven for surfers and water sports enthusiasts. Surf lessons cost around 10,000 XOF per hour.

Senegalese Cuisine: A Feast for the Senses

Food is central to Senegalese culture, and meals are often shared communally.

- **Must-Try Dishes**:
  - **Thieboudienne**: Senegal's national dish, a flavorful mix of rice, fish, and vegetables.
  - **Yassa**: A tangy chicken or fish dish marinated in onions and lemon.
  - **Bissap**: A refreshing hibiscus drink often served cold.
- **Cooking Classes**: Visitors can join classes in Dakar or Saint-Louis to learn how to prepare traditional dishes.

Spirituality and Religion

Senegal is predominantly Muslim, with a rich Sufi heritage that manifests in grand mosques and spiritual gatherings.

- **Touba**: Home to the **Grand Mosque of Touba**, a breathtaking architectural marvel and one of West Africa's most important religious sites.
- **Magal of Touba**: An annual pilgrimage celebrating Sheikh Amadou Bamba, attracting millions of worshippers.

Adventure and Outdoor Activities

For thrill-seekers, Senegal offers a range of activities:

- **Hiking**: Trails in the Casamance region and the Fouta Djallon offer breathtaking views and cultural encounters.
- **Kayaking**: Paddle through the mangroves of the Sine-Saloum Delta, where you can spot rare wildlife.
- **Quad Biking**: Explore the dunes surrounding Lac Rose or the desert landscapes near Lompoul.

Festivals and Celebrations

Senegal's festivals are a feast of color, music, and dance, reflecting its rich cultural diversity.

- **Saint-Louis Jazz Festival**: Held annually in May, it attracts world-class performers and celebrates Senegal's love for jazz.
- **Dakar Fashion Week**: A showcase of Senegalese and African talent in the fashion industry.

Accessibility and Convenience

Senegal is well-connected by flights, and its infrastructure is steadily improving. The **Blaise Diagne International Airport** in Dakar serves as the primary entry point. Regional flights and ferries make exploring the country easier, while a new toll road system reduces travel time significantly.

Quick Facts and Key Highlights

Essential Information for Travelers

- **Location**: Senegal, located on the westernmost tip of Africa, is bordered by the Atlantic Ocean to the west, Mauritania to the north, Mali to the east, and Guinea and Guinea-Bissau to the south.
- **Capital City**: Dakar, a vibrant cultural hub with historic and modern attractions.
- **Currency**: West African CFA Franc (XOF).
- **Language**: French (official); Wolof, Pulaar, and other indigenous languages widely spoken.
- **Timezone**: Greenwich Mean Time (GMT).

Key Attractions and Practical Details

1. **Gorée Island (Île de Gorée)**

   - **Address**: 2 km off the coast of Dakar. Accessible by ferry from the Port of Dakar.
   - **Opening Hours**: Daily, 9:00 AM - 6:00 PM.
   - **Ferry Price**: 5,200 XOF (approx. $8.50) for non-residents (round trip).
   - **Highlights**: The House of Slaves (Maison des Esclaves), historic colonial buildings, and cobblestone streets.
   - **Dining Options**: Try local seafood at "Chez Thiéo" or sip fresh juices at small beachfront cafes.
   - **Accommodation**: Boutique guesthouses such as "Maison Augustin Ly."

2. **Pink Lake (Lac Rose)**

   - **Address**: Retba, 30 km northeast of Dakar.

- Opening Hours: Open year-round; best viewed mid-morning or late afternoon.
- Entrance Fee: 3,000 XOF (approx. $5).
- Highlights: The lake's rosy hue caused by Dunaliella salina algae, salt harvesting, and dune buggy rides.
- Dining Options: Enjoy grilled fish at nearby roadside eateries.
- Accommodation: Stay at eco-lodges like "Le Trarza" for a rustic experience.

3. **Saint-Louis**
   - Address: Northern Senegal, 320 km from Dakar.
   - Opening Hours: Accessible daily.
   - Transport: Drive or take a bus from Dakar (5-6 hours).
   - Highlights: Colonial architecture, Faidherbe Bridge, and the annual Saint-Louis Jazz Festival.
   - Dining Options: Sample Saint-Louisienne cuisine at "La Linguère."
   - Accommodation: Heritage hotels like "Hotel de la Poste."

Senegal is a land of contrasts, blending natural wonders, vibrant cities, and deep historical roots. Its diversity caters to all types of travelers, from cultural enthusiasts to nature lovers. Below is a deeper dive into its key highlights:

Dakar: The Pulsating Heart of Senegal

Dakar is more than just Senegal's capital—it's a vibrant epicenter of culture, fashion, and innovation. The city's dynamic streets are a mix of traditional markets and contemporary art scenes.

- **Cultural Hotspots:**

- o **Museum of Black Civilizations**: A state-of-the-art museum celebrating African heritage.
  - o **Village des Arts**: A haven for local artists to showcase their works.
- **Beaches and Nightlife**:
- Dakar's coastline offers pristine beaches like **Ngor Island** and **Yoff Beach**, ideal for relaxation or surfing. The nightlife is equally enticing, with live music venues such as **Just4U** showcasing Senegal's iconic mbalax rhythms.

Sine-Saloum Delta: Senegal's Ecotourism Gem

This UNESCO-listed biosphere reserve is an intricate network of mangroves, salt flats, and islands.

- **Activities**:
  - o Kayaking through mangroves.
  - o Birdwatching for species like pelicans and flamingos.
  - o Visiting traditional Serer fishing villages.
- **Stay**: Experience authentic ecotourism at **Ecolodge de Palmarin**, a solar-powered retreat.

Casamance: A Hidden Tropical Paradise

The lush Casamance region in southern Senegal boasts a unique identity, influenced by its Diola traditions.

- **Ziguinchor**: The region's capital, known for its French colonial architecture and bustling markets.
- **Cap Skirring**: A beach haven offering luxurious resorts and secluded sands.
- **Cultural Immersion**: Witness Diola ceremonies or explore sacred groves in villages like Oussouye.

Cuisine: A Gastronomic Journey

Senegalese food is a flavorful blend of African, French, and Middle Eastern influences.

- **Signature Dishes**:
    - **Thieboudienne**: The national dish of rice, fish, and vegetables.
    - **Yassa**: Marinated chicken or fish in a tangy onion and lemon sauce.
    - **Café Touba**: A spiced coffee unique to Senegal.
- **Where to Eat**:
    - Upscale: **Le Lagon** in Dakar for fresh seafood.
    - Street Food: **Fataya** (fried pastries) from local vendors.

Festivals and Traditions

- **Grand Magal of Touba**: An annual religious pilgrimage to the holy city of Touba, celebrating the teachings of Sheikh Amadou Bamba.
- **Saint-Louis Jazz Festival**: A week-long event featuring global jazz talents.

Senegal is also famous for its griots, oral historians who preserve the nation's history through music and storytelling.

Geography and Climate Overview

Geography of Senegal: A Land of Contrasts

Senegal, perched on Africa's westernmost coast, is a geographic mosaic that melds vast plains, verdant river valleys, arid deserts, and shimmering coastlines. Its 196,722 square kilometers offer unique ecosystems shaped by the interplay of land and water. Understanding

Senegal's geography not only enriches your travels but deepens your appreciation of its rich cultural and ecological diversity.

1. **The Atlantic Coastline:**

   Senegal's coastal belt stretches over 531 kilometers along the Atlantic Ocean, offering scenic beaches, bustling fishing villages, and dynamic urban centers like Dakar. The Petite Côte, located south of Dakar, is renowned for its tranquil beach resorts, including Saly and Somone. Meanwhile, the Cap Vert Peninsula (home to Dakar) is Africa's westernmost point, flanked by dramatic cliffs and sandy coves.

   - **Highlight: Cap Skirring**, in the Casamance region, is an unspoiled paradise of golden sands fringed by lush palm trees.

2. **River Systems:**

   The country derives its name from the Senegal River, a vital waterway spanning 1,086 kilometers along the northern border with Mauritania. The Gambia River, another lifeline, traverses Senegal's southern regions, creating fertile lands and unique wetland ecosystems, such as the Sine-Saloum Delta—a UNESCO World Heritage site.

   - **Adventure Tip:** Boat safaris in the Sine-Saloum Delta offer encounters with manatees, dolphins, and exotic birdlife.

3. **The Sahel and Beyond:**

   Northern Senegal features semi-arid Sahel landscapes characterized by golden dunes and sparse vegetation. Saint-Louis, nestled near the Sahel region, showcases both colonial charm and a stark desert aesthetic.

   The Ferlo Valley, often overlooked by tourists, is a hub for nomadic Fulani herders and is punctuated by hardy acacia trees. This region exemplifies the resilience of Senegalese life amid challenging climates.

4. **Casamance: A Tropical Gem**

   The Casamance region, separated by The Gambia, offers a lush contrast to the arid north. It is defined by rainforests, rice paddies, and a network of rivers and creeks. Its capital, Ziguinchor, is an excellent base for exploring local Diola culture.

   o **Highlight:** The mangroves of Casamance are best explored by kayak, with local guides providing insight into the area's biodiversity.

Climate: Patterns that Shape Senegal's Life

Senegal's climate is defined by its tropical latitude and proximity to the Atlantic. The country experiences two distinct seasons: the dry season (November to May) and the wet season (June to October).

1. **The Dry Season:**

   Dominated by the Harmattan winds blowing from the Sahara, the dry season features clear skies, mild temperatures, and minimal rainfall. This is the peak travel period, especially for coastal destinations like Dakar and Saint-Louis.

   o **Tip:** Pack light cotton clothing and sunscreen; Harmattan winds can also make the air dusty.

2. **The Wet Season:**

   The rains begin in June, intensifying by August and tapering off in October. Southern regions like Casamance receive more rainfall than the north, turning the landscape into a vibrant green tapestry. However, flooding can impact travel in rural areas.

- o **Highlight:** The wet season transforms Djoudj Bird Sanctuary into a haven for migratory birds, including flamingos and pelicans.

3. **Regional Variations:**
   - o **Coastal Areas:** Enjoy cooler temperatures (20°C–30°C) year-round due to the Atlantic's moderating influence.
   - o **Interior Regions:** Expect hotter conditions, especially in the Sahel and Ferlo Valley, where temperatures can soar to 40°C in peak summer.
   - o **Casamance:** A humid, tropical microclimate prevails, making it ideal for agriculture and lush biodiversity.

Unique Geographical Features

1. **Pink Lake (Lac Rose):**

   The lake's bubblegum hue results from algae reacting to high salt levels, creating a surreal landscape against the backdrop of white salt mounds. Its saline waters rival those of the Dead Sea, making it a popular site for therapeutic floatation experiences.

2. **Baobab Forests:**

   Known as the "Tree of Life," baobabs dominate Senegal's savannas, serving as symbols of resilience and cultural significance. The Forest of the Sacred Baobabs near Joal-Fadiouth is particularly noteworthy, with ancient trees revered in local folklore.

3. **Fathala Wildlife Reserve:**

   Located in the Sine-Saloum region, this reserve offers a safari experience with lions, giraffes, and other wildlife roaming freely amid savannas and wetlands.

Travel Tip: Integrating Geography and Climate into Your Trip

- **For Coastal Enthusiasts:** Plan visits during the dry season for optimal beach weather and water sports.

- **For Birdwatchers and Ecotourists:** Visit during the wet season when bird sanctuaries like Djoudj and Sine-Saloum Delta are teeming with life.

- **For Cultural Explorers:** Northern regions like Saint-Louis blend history with unique Sahel landscapes, best visited from November to February for comfortable temperatures.

Historical and Cultural Significance

Senegal's history is rich and multifaceted, shaped by ancient empires, trans-Saharan trade routes, colonial rule, and its eventual independence. The country has been a crossroads of cultures, serving as a vital link between North Africa, West Africa, and Europe.

Ancient Kingdoms and Early Civilizations

- **Kingdom of Tekrur (9th–12th centuries):** One of the earliest known West African states, Tekrur emerged in the Senegal River valley. It played a key role in spreading Islam in the region through its connections with North African Berber traders.

- **The Jolof Empire (13th–16th centuries):** A powerful confederation of Wolof-speaking states, the Jolof Empire was known for its strong centralized governance and thriving trade networks. Goods like gold, ivory, and slaves were traded, linking Senegal to larger global economies.

Notable Site: Sine Ngayene Stone Circles (Joal-Fadiouth)

- **Address:** Near Joal-Fadiouth, Fatick Region
- **Opening Times:** Daily, 8:00 AM – 6:00 PM
- **Entry Fee:** Around $5 USD

17

- **Details:** This UNESCO World Heritage Site consists of thousands of megalithic stone circles believed to mark ancient burial grounds dating back over 2,000 years. Visitors can learn about the area's pre-Islamic and pre-colonial history.

The Transatlantic Slave Trade

Senegal was deeply affected by the transatlantic slave trade, with Gorée Island being one of the most infamous transit points.

- **Gorée Island:** Located just off Dakar, this UNESCO World Heritage Site was a hub for the slave trade from the 15th to the 19th century.
    - **Address:** Gorée Island, accessed via ferry from Dakar
    - **Ferry Timings:** Daily departures every hour from 7:30 AM to 6:30 PM
    - **Ferry Ticket Price:** $6 USD (round trip)
    - **Entry Fee to the House of Slaves:** $3 USD
    - **Highlights:** Visit the House of Slaves (Maison des Esclaves), where the "Door of No Return" symbolizes the departure of millions of enslaved Africans. Guides provide poignant narratives of the trade's impact.

Colonial Era and Independence

Senegal was a French colony from the mid-17th century until it achieved independence in 1960.

- **Saint-Louis:** The first French settlement in West Africa and the capital of Senegal until 1902. It is known for its colonial architecture and cultural festivals.
    - **Address:** Saint-Louis, accessible by road or domestic flights
    - **Opening Times:** Attractions like the Faidherbe Bridge are open year-round

- o **Pricing:** Free to explore most public areas
- o **Highlights:** Stroll through the narrow streets of Saint-Louis Island, visit the colonial-era Governor's Palace, and enjoy its lively jazz festival every May.

Post-Independence Legacy: Under the leadership of Léopold Sédar Senghor, Senegal became a beacon of African cultural and political identity. Senghor, a poet and intellectual, promoted the concept of *Négritude*, celebrating African heritage and identity.

Cultural Significance

1. **Language and Oral Traditions**

    Senegal is a multilingual society with over 36 languages spoken. Wolof is the lingua franca, though French remains the official language.

- **Griots:** Traditional storytellers, known as *griots*, are the custodians of Senegal's oral history. They preserve genealogies, historical events, and moral lessons through songs and narratives.
    - o **Where to Experience:**
        - **Dakar's Village des Arts:** Features griot performances on select evenings.
            - **Address:** Route de Rufisque, Dakar
            - **Opening Times:** Tuesday to Sunday, 10:00 AM – 7:00 PM
            - **Entry Fee:** Free, donations encouraged

2. Music and Dance

Senegal is the birthplace of *mbalax*, a popular music genre blending traditional sabar drumming with global influences like jazz and rock.

- **Notable Artists:** Youssou N'Dour and Baaba Maal have brought Senegalese music to international fame.

- **Cultural Centers to Visit:**
  - **Théâtre National Daniel Sorano (Dakar):** Offers live music and dance performances.
    - **Address:** Avenue Cheikh Anta Diop, Dakar
    - **Opening Times:** Performance schedules vary
    - **Pricing:** Tickets range from $10–$25 USD

3. Festivals and Celebrations

- **Saint-Louis Jazz Festival:** One of Africa's premier music festivals, held every May.
  - **Address:** Various venues across Saint-Louis
  - **Entry Fees:** Ticket prices vary depending on performances
- **Dak'Art Biennale:** A major contemporary art festival showcasing African creativity.
  - **Address:** Multiple galleries and public spaces in Dakar
  - **Timing:** Held biennially in May
  - **Pricing:** Free entry to most exhibitions

4. Religion and Spiritual Practices

Islam is the dominant religion, with approximately 95% of the population identifying as Muslim. Senegalese Islam is uniquely intertwined with Sufi brotherhoods, such as the Mourides and Tijaniyyas.

- **Mouride Brotherhood:**
  - **Touba and the Great Mosque:** A pilgrimage site and the spiritual heart of the Mouride community.
    - **Address:** Touba, 194 km from Dakar
    - **Opening Times:** Open daily, 24 hours

- **Pricing:** Free entry
- **Details:** The mosque features intricate marble designs and is one of the largest in Africa.
- **Christian Influence:** A small but significant Christian community exists, with striking cathedrals like the Dakar Cathedral (Cathédrale Notre-Dame des Victoires).

5.Culinary Traditions

Senegal's cuisine reflects its history, blending local, North African, and French influences.

- **Signature Dishes:**
  - **Thieboudienne:** Senegal's national dish made with rice, fish, and vegetables.
  - **Yassa:** A tangy dish of chicken or fish marinated in lemon and onions.
- **Recommended Dining:**
  - **Chez Loutcha (Dakar):** Known for authentic Senegalese dishes.
    - **Address:** 101 Rue Moussé Diop, Dakar
    - **Opening Times:** Daily, 11:00 AM – 11:00 PM
    - **Pricing:** Dishes start at $10 USD

Language and Local Etiquette

Wolof and French: The Linguistic Landscape

Senegal is a linguistic mosaic where over 30 languages are spoken, reflecting its diverse ethnic tapestry. While **French** serves as the official language and is used in government, education, and formal settings, **Wolof** is the lingua franca spoken by nearly everyone, regardless of ethnic background.

Ethnic Languages: Beyond Wolof, languages like **Pulaar**, **Serer**, and **Diola** are regionally dominant. For instance, if you travel to the Casamance region, you'll encounter the Diola language, whereas the northern regions predominantly use Pulaar.

Practical Use of Language

While French may suffice in urban areas and tourist hubs, a few words in Wolof can go a long way in breaking barriers and creating genuine connections.

Regional Differences in Language Use

Each region in Senegal has its unique linguistic charm. While Dakar is a melting pot of Wolof and French, visiting Saint-Louis offers a glimpse into French colonial influence through its language and architecture. In contrast, the Casamance region prides itself on its Diola heritage.

Local Etiquette in Senegal

Greeting Rituals: A Sign of Respect

In Senegal, greetings are more than polite exchanges—they are a social cornerstone. Upon meeting someone, it's customary to ask about their well-being and that of their family. The process can seem lengthy to outsiders, but skipping it is considered rude.

Respect for Elders and Hierarchies

Senegalese society places significant emphasis on respecting elders and authority figures. When interacting with someone older, use formal language and avoid interrupting. Offering a small gesture of respect, such as yielding a seat or letting them speak first, is appreciated.

Hospitality: Teranga in Action

The Senegalese concept of **Teranga** (hospitality) is legendary. Visitors are treated as honored guests, often with meals, tea ceremonies, or gifts. When invited into a home:

- Remove your shoes at the entrance.
- Accept food or drink offered—it's a sign of respect and appreciation.
- If eating from a communal bowl, use your right hand, as the left is reserved for less sanitary tasks.

Dress Code and Modesty

While Dakar and tourist hubs are more relaxed, rural areas and religious sites require modest attire. Women should avoid short skirts or sleeveless tops, while men should opt for shirts and trousers instead of shorts.

Religious Sensitivity: Senegal is predominantly Muslim, and Fridays are significant prayer days. Avoid scheduling meetings or loud activities during midday prayers.

Public Behavior and Gestures

- **Physical Affection:** Public displays of affection, such as kissing or hugging, are generally frowned upon, especially in conservative areas.
- **Pointing:** Avoid pointing at people directly; instead, gesture with your entire hand.
- **Photographs:** Always ask for permission before taking pictures of locals, especially in rural or sensitive areas.

Dining Etiquette

Traditional Meals and Sharing

Senegalese meals often involve communal dining from a large shared bowl. The host might serve guests from the choicest portions of the dish. Avoid reaching beyond your immediate section of the bowl.

Tea Ceremony (Attaya): After meals, a three-round tea ceremony is customary. It symbolizes friendship and hospitality. Each round is progressively sweeter, signifying life's journey from bitterness to sweetness.

Addressing Locations and Pricing

Example Dining Spots:

1. **La Fourchette, Dakar**
   - **Address:** Avenue Cheikh Anta Diop, Dakar
   - **Opening Times:** 12 PM – 11 PM daily
   - **Pricing:** $20–$40 per meal

2. **Chez Loutcha, Saint-Louis**
   - **Address:** Place Faidherbe, Saint-Louis
   - **Opening Times:** 11 AM – 10 PM
   - **Pricing:** $10–$20

3. **Le Kora, Saly**
   - **Address:** Route de Saly, Petite Côte
   - **Opening Times:** 7 AM – 11 PM
   - **Pricing:** $15–$35

Essential Travel Tips

1. Entry Requirements and Visas

Most visitors require a valid passport to enter Senegal. Some nationalities may need a visa, while others can visit visa-free for up to 90 days. Always check specific requirements based on your nationality. Senegal's main entry point is **Blaise Diagne International Airport (DSS)**, located 43 km from Dakar.

2. Local Transportation

- **Taxis**: Taxis are abundant but not metered. Always agree on a fare before beginning your journey. In Dakar, fares typically range from XOF 1,000 to XOF 3,000 depending on the distance.

- **Buses and Minibuses (Ndiaga Ndiaye)**: These are budget-friendly options for local transport but are often crowded and less reliable.
- **Car Rentals**: Available in Dakar and major cities for those seeking more independence. Roads are generally good, but rural areas may require a 4x4 vehicle.

3. Top Attractions in Senegal

1. **Gorée Island (Île de Gorée)**
   - **Address**: Off the coast of Dakar, accessible via ferry from Dakar Port.
   - **Opening Hours**: Daily, 9:00 AM - 6:00 PM.
   - **Pricing**: Ferry: XOF 5,200 round trip; Museum fees: XOF 500 - XOF 2,000.
   - **Description**: A UNESCO World Heritage Site, Gorée Island is a poignant reminder of the transatlantic slave trade. The *Maison des Esclaves* (House of Slaves) and its "Door of No Return" evoke profound emotions, while the island's cobbled streets, vibrant art galleries, and quaint cafes offer opportunities for reflection and relaxation.

2. **Pink Lake (Lac Rose)**
   - **Address**: 30 km northeast of Dakar.
   - **Opening Hours**: Open year-round. Guided tours recommended during daylight hours.
   - **Pricing**: Guided tours start at XOF 10,000 per person.
   - **Description**: This saltwater lake turns a stunning pink hue due to its high salinity and algae content. Visitors can float effortlessly in its dense waters, take a guided boat tour, or explore nearby salt harvesting operations.

3. **Niokolo-Koba National Park**
   - **Address**: Southeastern Senegal, near Tambacounda.

- **Opening Hours**: Dry season (November - May) is ideal for wildlife viewing.
- **Pricing**: Entry fee: XOF 10,000; Safari tours: Starting at XOF 25,000 per person.
- **Description**: A UNESCO Biosphere Reserve, this park is home to lions, elephants, antelope, and hundreds of bird species. Guided safaris are essential for a safe and enriching experience.

4. Dining in Senegal

Senegal's cuisine is a delightful fusion of African, French, and Middle Eastern influences, with an emphasis on fresh seafood and locally grown produce.

1. **Thieboudienne**: The national dish, made of fish, rice, and vegetables cooked in a tomato-based sauce.
2. **Yassa Poulet**: Chicken marinated in onions, lemon, and mustard, served with rice.
3. **Local Drinks**: Try *bissap* (hibiscus juice) and *gingembre* (ginger juice).

Recommended Dining Spots:

- **La Fourchette (Dakar)**: Renowned for its fusion of French and Senegalese cuisine.
  - **Address**: 4 Rue Parent, Dakar.
  - **Opening Hours**: Daily, 12:00 PM - 11:00 PM.
  - **Pricing**: Meals range from XOF 8,000 - XOF 20,000.
- **Chez Loutcha (Saint-Louis)**: Known for hearty portions of traditional dishes.

5. Accommodation in Senegal

1. **Luxury Options**

- King Fahd Palace Hotel (Dakar): Offers stunning ocean views, fine dining, and a serene poolside retreat.
  - Pricing: Starting at XOF 120,000 per night.

2. **Eco-Friendly Stays**
   - **Ecolodge de Palmarin (Sine-Saloum Delta)**: Ideal for nature lovers, surrounded by mangroves and wildlife.
     - **Pricing**: Starting at XOF 40,000 per night.

3. **Budget-Friendly Options**
   - **Auberge Keur Diame (Dakar)**: A cozy, family-run guesthouse with a personal touch.
     - **Pricing**: Starting at XOF 10,000 per night.

6. Cultural Etiquette and Tips

1. **Greetings**: Always greet people with a handshake or a friendly "Salaam Aleikum" (peace be upon you).
2. **Dress Modestly**: While Senegal is relatively liberal, modest clothing is appreciated, especially in rural areas.
3. **Photography**: Always ask permission before photographing people, particularly in rural communities.
4. **Gift-Giving**: Small gifts, such as tea or sweets, are appreciated when visiting local families.

7. Health and Safety

- **Vaccinations**: Yellow fever vaccination is mandatory. Consider vaccines for hepatitis A, typhoid, and malaria prophylaxis.
- **Water**: Drink only bottled or filtered water to avoid illness.
- **Safety**: Petty theft can occur in busy areas, so keep valuables secure.

By incorporating these tips and insights, you'll be well-prepared to explore Senegal's unique blend of history, culture, and natural beauty.

CHAPTER 2.

PLANNING YOUR TRIP

Senegal's diverse geography, vibrant culture, and unique ecosystems make it a year-round destination. However, understanding its distinct seasons and how they affect travel experiences is crucial for making the most of your visit. This guide provides an in-depth look at Senegal's climatic variations, cultural events, and seasonal attractions to help you determine the best time to plan your trip.

Best Time to Visit Senegal

Senegal experiences two main seasons:

1. **Dry Season (November to May)**
   - Characterized by clear skies, cooler temperatures, and minimal rainfall.
   - Average temperatures range from 24°C (75°F) on the coast to 30°C (86°F) inland.

2. **Rainy Season (June to October)**
   - Marked by short but intense rainfalls, higher humidity, and lush green landscapes.
   - Average temperatures range from 26°C (79°F) on the coast to 35°C (95°F) inland.

Month-by-Month Breakdown of the Best Times to Visit

November to February: The Peak Tourist Season

- **Why Visit?**
  - Cool, dry weather is ideal for exploring cities, national parks, and beaches.
  - The Harmattan winds bring a pleasant, dry breeze.
  - Perfect time for wildlife viewing, as animals gather around water sources.
- **Key Attractions and Events**
  - **Djoudj Bird Sanctuary**: This UNESCO World Heritage Site near Saint-Louis is teeming with migratory birds, including pelicans and flamingos.
    - **Opening Hours**: Daily, 8:00 AM - 5:30 PM
    - **Pricing**: XOF 5,000 per person (guided tours extra).
  - **Saint-Louis Jazz Festival**: Held in February, this iconic event showcases world-class jazz performances in a historic colonial setting.
    - **Tickets**: Starting at XOF 10,000 per event.
- **Accommodation and Dining Recommendations**
  - **Hotel de la Poste (Saint-Louis)**: A charming hotel with colonial architecture.
    - **Pricing**: XOF 45,000 per night.
  - **Restaurant Teranga (Dakar)**: Offers traditional Senegalese dishes with a modern twist.
    - **Pricing**: Meals range from XOF 6,000 to XOF 15,000.

March to May: Shoulder Season

- **Why Visit?**
  - Fewer tourists and moderate weather make this a great time for those seeking a quieter experience.
  - Ideal for cultural tours and exploring rural regions like Casamance before the rains begin.
- **Key Attractions and Events**
  - **Sine-Saloum Delta**: Known for its mangroves, birdlife, and serene beauty. Perfect for kayaking or boat tours.
    - **Opening Hours**: Accessible daily; best explored with a guide.
    - **Pricing**: Guided tours start at XOF 10,000 per person.
- **Accommodation and Dining Recommendations**
  - **Campement Keur Bamboung (Sine-Saloum Delta)**: An eco-friendly lodge surrounded by nature.
    - **Pricing**: XOF 35,000 per night, including meals.

June to October: Rainy Season

- **Why Visit?**
  - Despite the rain, this is the best time to witness Senegal's lush greenery and agricultural vibrancy.
  - Ideal for cultural immersion in regions like Casamance, where rain revitalizes the landscape.
- **Key Attractions and Events**
  - **Casamance Region**: Explore Ziguinchor and nearby villages like Cap Skirring. The rain transforms the region into a tropical paradise.
    - **Opening Hours**: Accessible year-round.

- - **Pricing**: Local tours start at XOF 8,000.
- **Special Note**: Mosquitoes are more prevalent during this time, so pack insect repellent and wear long sleeves in the evenings.
- **Accommodation and Dining Recommendations**
  - **Les Alizés Beach Resort (Cap Skirring)**: A luxury beachside retreat offering spa services.
    - **Pricing**: Starting at XOF 90,000 per night.
  - **Chez Katia (Ziguinchor)**: Renowned for its hearty West African meals.
    - **Pricing**: Meals range from XOF 4,000 to XOF 10,000.

Factors to Consider When Choosing the Best Time

1. **Purpose of Visit**
   - **Wildlife Watching**: November to February for migratory birds and animals.
   - **Cultural Experiences**: Attend festivals like the Jazz Festival in Saint-Louis (February) or Tabaski (varies with the lunar calendar).
   - **Relaxation**: Cap Skirring's beaches are most tranquil in March and April.
2. **Budget**
   - Traveling during the rainy season (low season) offers significant savings on accommodations and tours.
3. **Health Precautions**
   - The rainy season increases the risk of malaria. Ensure you take preventive measures, including prophylactic medications and sleeping under mosquito nets.

Visa and Entry Requirements

Overview of Visa Policy

Visa Exemptions

Senegal offers visa-free entry to citizens of many countries, particularly within Africa and Europe, as well as a few from Asia and the Americas. Visitors from these nations can stay for up to 90 days without requiring a visa.

- **Countries Exempt from Visas:**
- Citizens of ECOWAS (Economic Community of West African States) member countries, including Nigeria, Ghana, and Côte d'Ivoire, can travel visa-free.
- European countries such as France, Germany, Italy, and the United Kingdom are also visa-exempt.
- Certain Asian countries, including Japan and South Korea, qualify for visa-free entry.

E-Visa and Visa on Arrival

For travelers not eligible for visa-free entry, Senegal introduced an e-visa system for convenience. This system allows applicants to apply online before their travel. In exceptional cases, some travelers may obtain a visa on arrival, though prior arrangements are recommended to avoid delays.

Visa Types and Applications

Tourist Visa

- **Purpose**: For leisure travel and short-term visits, typically up to 90 days.
- **Application Requirements:**
  - Valid passport with at least six months of validity beyond the date of entry.

- Completed visa application form (available online or at the Senegalese embassy).
- Recent passport-sized photographs (2).
- Proof of accommodation (hotel reservation or invitation letter from a host).
- Return or onward flight ticket.
- Proof of sufficient funds for the duration of your stay.

Business Visa

- **Purpose**: For professionals attending meetings, conferences, or engaging in commercial activities.
- **Additional Documents**:
  - Letter of invitation from the Senegalese company or organization.
  - Evidence of the purpose of the trip (conference registration, business correspondence).

Transit Visa

- **Purpose**: For travelers transiting through Senegal to another destination.
- **Validity**: Usually valid for a stay of up to 72 hours.
- **Key Requirement**: Confirmed onward travel tickets.

How to Apply for a Senegal Visa

Step 1: Determine Eligibility

Verify whether your nationality requires a visa or qualifies for visa-free entry. If you are eligible for an e-visa, proceed with the online application process.

Step 2: Gather Necessary Documents

Compile all required documentation based on the visa type. Ensure that all information provided matches your travel itinerary and passport details.

Step 3: Submit the Application

- **For E-Visa Applications**:
    - o Visit the official e-visa portal of Senegal.
    - o Fill out the online application form with accurate details.
    - o Upload required documents in the specified format.
    - o Pay the visa fee online using a valid credit or debit card. Fees typically range between $50 and $100, depending on the visa type.
- **For Embassy Applications**:
    - o Locate the nearest Senegalese embassy or consulate.
    - o Submit the application form and supporting documents in person or by mail, as required.

Step 4: Await Approval

- E-visas are usually processed within 5-7 business days. Embassy processing times may vary but generally take 10-15 working days.

Step 5: Receive and Verify Visa

Once approved, ensure that all details on the visa are correct, including your name, passport number, and travel dates.

Visa Fees and Associated Costs

- **Tourist Visa**: $50 to $80 (varies by nationality and application method).
- **Business Visa**: $80 to $120.

- **Transit Visa**: $30 to $50.

Additional charges may apply for expedited processing or courier services for embassy applications.

Key Entry Points and Border Crossings

Blaise Diagne International Airport (DSS)

- **Location**: 43 km from Dakar.
- **Opening Hours**: Open 24/7.
- **Facilities**: Visa services, customs, and duty-free shops.

Land Borders

- **Key Crossings**:
    - Senegal-Gambia border (Amdallai/Karang checkpoint).
    - Senegal-Mauritania border (Rosso crossing).

Travelers entering through land borders must carry the necessary visa and documentation, as facilities may be limited compared to airports.

Special Considerations

Passport Validity

Ensure your passport is valid for at least six months beyond your intended departure date. Some airlines and immigration authorities may deny boarding or entry if this requirement is not met.

Travel with Children

If traveling with minors, carry additional documents, including:

- Birth certificates.
- Consent letters from non-accompanying parents or guardians.

Yellow Fever Vaccination Certificate

Senegal mandates proof of yellow fever vaccination for all travelers over nine months old. Carry an international vaccination certificate, as it may be checked at entry points.

Customs Regulations

- **Prohibited Items**: Illegal drugs, unlicensed firearms, and pornography are strictly banned.
- **Duty-Free Allowance**: Visitors may bring in reasonable quantities of personal items, alcohol (1 liter), and tobacco (200 cigarettes or equivalent).

Common Challenges and How to Overcome Them

1. **Delayed Approvals**: Apply well in advance, ideally 4-6 weeks before your travel date, to avoid last-minute issues.
2. **Incomplete Documentation**: Double-check all documents before submission to ensure a seamless application process.
3. **Language Barriers**: While French is the official language, embassy staff and immigration officers are generally proficient in English.

Extending Your Stay

Tourists wishing to stay beyond 90 days must apply for an extension at the **Department of Immigration in Dakar**.

- **Address**: Route de l'Aéroport, Dakar.
- **Opening Hours**: Monday to Friday, 8:00 AM - 4:00 PM.
- **Fees**: XOF 20,000 to XOF 40,000 depending on the extension duration.

Health and Safety Tips

1. Vaccinations and Preventive Care

Before traveling to Senegal, certain vaccinations and medications are crucial:

1. **Yellow Fever Vaccine**
   - **Requirement**: Mandatory for entry.

- o **Cost**: Approximately $50 - $150, depending on the clinic.
- o Ensure you carry an International Certificate of Vaccination (yellow card).

2. **Recommended Vaccines**
   - o **Hepatitis A and B**: Essential for protection against contaminated food and water or medical procedures.
   - o **Typhoid**: Necessary if you plan to eat or drink outside major hotels or restaurants.
   - o **Rabies**: Consider if you plan to engage in outdoor activities or are visiting rural areas.

3. **Malaria Prophylaxis**
   - o Senegal is a malaria-endemic country. Speak with a travel doctor about preventive medication such as doxycycline or atovaquone-proguanil.

4. **Routine Vaccinations**
   - o Ensure your tetanus, measles-mumps-rubella (MMR), and polio vaccinations are up-to-date.

2. Water and Food Safety

1. **Drinking Water**
   - o Tap water in Senegal is not safe for consumption. Always opt for bottled or filtered water.
   - o **Brands Available**: Kirène and O'Cool. Prices range from XOF 500 - XOF 1,000 for a 1.5-liter bottle.

2. **Street Food Safety**
   - o Senegal's street food is tempting but take precautions. Opt for freshly prepared dishes like *beignets* (fried

doughnuts) or grilled fish. Avoid raw or undercooked foods.

3. **Dining in Restaurants**
   - Stick to reputable establishments:
     - **Le Djembé (Dakar)**
       - **Address**: Rue Jules Ferry, Plateau, Dakar.
       - **Opening Hours**: Daily, 11:00 AM - 11:00 PM.
       - **Pricing**: Meals range from XOF 8,000 - XOF 20,000.
       - **Specialty**: Offers delicious and hygienic Senegalese cuisine.

3. Medical Emergencies and Pharmacies

1. **Emergency Contacts**
   - Police: 17
   - Ambulance: 15
   - Fire Brigade (also provides medical assistance): 18

2. **Pharmacies**
   - Pharmacies are widely available in major cities like Dakar, Saint-Louis, and Ziguinchor. Look for signs with a green cross.
   - **Pharmacie Guigon** (Dakar)
     - **Address**: Avenue Cheikh Anta Diop, Dakar.
     - **Opening Hours**: 24/7.

3. **What to Pack in a Travel Health Kit**
   - Antimalarials and fever-reducing medications.

- o Oral rehydration salts (ORS) for dehydration.
- o Antihistamines for allergies.
- o Band-aids, antiseptic cream, and tweezers for minor injuries.

4. Navigating Senegal Safely

1. City Safety

- o Dakar is generally safe, but petty theft can occur. Keep valuables secure, especially in crowded areas like Sandaga Market.
- o Avoid walking alone at night, particularly in unfamiliar neighborhoods.

2. Rural and Wildlife Areas

- o Exercise caution when exploring rural areas or national parks. Always use a registered guide for safaris or hikes.
- o In the Sine-Saloum Delta or Casamance, respect local wildlife and adhere to park regulations.

5. Transportation Safety

1. Taxis

- o Avoid unregistered taxis; opt for brightly painted yellow taxis in Dakar.
- o Always agree on a fare before starting your trip.

2. Buses and Minibuses

- o While affordable, these can be overcrowded and lack proper maintenance. For longer journeys, consider private minibuses (referred to as *sept-places*).

3. Driving in Senegal

- o Road conditions are generally good in urban areas but can be challenging in rural regions. Avoid nighttime driving due to poorly lit roads and stray animals.

6. Environmental and Weather Hazards

1. **Heat and Sun Protection**
   - o Senegal has a tropical climate; temperatures can soar above 40°C (104°F) during the dry season.
   - o Use high-SPF sunscreen, wear breathable clothing, and stay hydrated.

2. **Rainy Season (June - October)**
   - o Heavy rains may cause flooding in low-lying areas. Avoid traveling during this time if you're not accustomed to such conditions.

7. Cultural Etiquette and Safety

1. **Respect Local Customs**
   - o Dress modestly, especially when visiting religious sites such as mosques.
   - o Avoid public displays of affection, as Senegal is a predominantly Muslim country.

2. **Interacting with Locals**
   - o Greet with "Salaam Aleikum" and engage with locals respectfully. Learning basic Wolof phrases can go a long way in fostering goodwill.

3. **Scams and Touts**
   - o Be cautious of overly persistent street vendors or offers that seem too good to be true.

8. Wildlife and Nature Precautions

1. **Insect Protection**

- o Mosquito-borne diseases like malaria are prevalent. Use insect repellent containing DEET and sleep under treated mosquito nets.

2. **Animal Encounters**
   - o In parks like Niokolo-Koba, observe wildlife from a safe distance. Never attempt to feed or touch animals.

3. **Marine Hazards**
   - o Be mindful of strong currents and jellyfish stings when swimming in the Atlantic. Always swim in designated areas.

9. Traveler Insurance and Documentation

- Purchase comprehensive travel insurance that covers medical emergencies, theft, and cancellations.
- Carry copies of important documents, including your passport, visa, and insurance details.

What to Pack: Essential Items for Senegal

1. Clothing

Senegal's climate varies by region but is generally tropical, with a hot and humid rainy season (June to October) and a dry season (November to May). Packing versatile, lightweight clothing is key.

1. **Lightweight, Breathable Clothing**
   - o Opt for cotton, linen, or moisture-wicking materials to stay cool.
   - o Long-sleeved shirts and pants are essential for protecting against mosquitoes in the evenings and during safaris.

2. **Modest Clothing**
   - o Senegal is a predominantly Muslim country, and modest dress is respectful, especially in rural areas. Women should consider packing knee-length skirts or dresses and shawls for covering shoulders.

3. **Beachwear**
   - o Swimsuits are fine for beaches like Saly or Popenguine, but avoid overly revealing attire.
   - o A cover-up or sarong is helpful for walking to and from the beach.

4. **Rain Gear (Seasonal)**
   - o If traveling during the rainy season, pack a lightweight, waterproof jacket and an umbrella.

5. **Comfortable Shoes**
   - o Sturdy walking shoes or hiking boots for nature reserves and treks.
   - o Sandals or flip-flops for beaches and casual outings.

2. Travel Documents and Essentials

1. **Passport and Visa**
   - o Ensure your passport has at least six months' validity.
   - o If required, secure your visa in advance and carry a printed copy.

2. **Travel Insurance Documents**
   - o Include coverage for medical emergencies, trip cancellations, and lost belongings.

3. **Vaccination Card**
   - o Yellow fever vaccination is mandatory. Keep your international vaccination card accessible.

4. **Copies of Important Documents**
   - o Photocopy your passport, visa, and travel insurance policy. Keep these separate from the originals.

3. Health and Hygiene Supplies

1. **Mosquito Repellent**
   - o Use a repellent containing DEET or picaridin to prevent bites, especially in areas with malaria risk.

2. **Sunscreen**
   - o Choose SPF 30 or higher, as Senegal's sun can be intense, even during cooler months.

3. **First Aid Kit**
   - o Include bandages, antiseptic wipes, pain relievers, antihistamines, and anti-diarrheal medication.

4. **Reusable Water Bottle**
   - o Opt for one with a built-in filter to ensure safe drinking water while reducing plastic waste.

5. **Personal Hygiene Products**
   - o Bring travel-sized toiletries, wet wipes, and hand sanitizer.
   - o For women, menstrual supplies can be scarce in rural areas; pack accordingly.

4. Electronics and Gadgets

1. **Universal Travel Adapter**
   - o Senegal uses 230V electricity with Type C and E plugs. A universal adapter ensures compatibility.

2. **Power Bank**
   - o Useful for recharging devices during long journeys or in remote areas.

3. **Smartphone and Apps**
   - Pre-download maps, translation apps, and offline guides.
   - Local SIM cards (e.g., Orange or Free) provide affordable data plans.
4. **Camera**
   - Bring a high-quality camera or smartphone with ample storage for capturing Senegal's landscapes and culture.

5. Specific Items for Activities

1. **Safari and Nature Excursions**
   - Binoculars for wildlife spotting in Niokolo-Koba National Park or Djoudj Bird Sanctuary.
   - Neutral-colored clothing to blend into the environment and avoid alarming animals.
2. **Beach Days**
   - Waterproof bag for protecting electronics.
   - Snorkeling gear if visiting marine-rich areas like the Petite Côte.
3. **Cultural and Urban Exploration**
   - A lightweight scarf or shawl can serve multiple purposes: covering up in religious sites, protecting against dust, or as a sunshade.

6. Local Currency and Financial Preparations

1. **Cash and Cards**
   - Carry West African CFA Francs (XOF) for smaller vendors and tips. Larger establishments in cities accept credit cards.
2. **Money Belt**

- A discreet money belt can secure cash and documents when traveling through crowded markets like Sandaga in Dakar.

3. **ATMs and Exchange Rates**
     - ATMs are available in major cities but may charge foreign transaction fees. Consider exchanging money at reputable bureaus.

Additional Packing Tips

1. **Cultural Sensitivity**
     - Pack small gifts, like local sweets or tea, if you anticipate visiting local families. It's a warm gesture of appreciation.

2. **Reusable Items**
     - Reusable shopping bags are practical for markets and eco-friendly.

3. **Language Tools**
     - A pocket phrasebook with basic French and Wolof phrases can enhance interactions and show respect for the local culture.

Accommodation-Specific Items

- If staying in eco-lodges or rural guesthouses, bring a portable mosquito net and extra batteries for flashlights.
- For upscale hotels, such as the **Radisson Blu Dakar Sea Plaza**, packing a stylish outfit for evening dining or events is recommended.
     - **Address**: Route de la Corniche Ouest, Dakar.
     - **Pricing**: Rooms start at XOF 120,000 per night.

Dining-Specific Items

- Pack reusable utensils, such as travel cutlery or chopsticks, to enjoy street food in places like **Soumbédioune Market** in Dakar.
    - **Opening Hours**: 9:00 AM – 7:00 PM.
    - **Specialty**: Freshly grilled seafood.

Cultural Do's and Don'ts

Do's in Senegalese Culture

1. Greet People Properly

- **Cultural Context**: Greetings are an essential part of Senegalese interaction, reflecting respect and connection.
- **What to Do**: Begin with "Salaam Aleikum" (peace be upon you), and expect the response, "Aleikum Salaam." Add inquiries about the person's health, family, and well-being.
- **Tip**: When meeting elders, use both hands or slightly bow to show deference.

2. Dress Modestly

- **Cultural Context**: While Senegal is relatively liberal, conservative attire reflects respect for Islamic values, especially in rural areas.
- **What to Wear**: Loose-fitting clothing that covers shoulders and knees. Women may want to carry a scarf for visiting religious sites.
- **Special Note**: In urban hubs like Dakar, modern clothing is acceptable, but avoid overly revealing outfits.

3. Participate in Cultural Practices

- **Key Practices**:

- o Sharing tea (*attaya*) is a symbol of friendship. Accepting a cup builds trust and rapport.
  - o Dancing to traditional music like *mbalax* is not only welcomed but celebrated.
- **Tip**: If invited to a ceremony, such as a wedding or naming event, attend! Bring a small gift, such as sugar, tea, or money, as a gesture of goodwill.

4. Respect Elders and Authority Figures

- **Cultural Context**: Senegalese society places a strong emphasis on hierarchy and respect.
- **What to Do**: Stand when an elder enters the room and use formal titles like "Tonton" (uncle) or "Tata" (aunt) even for non-relatives.

5. Support Local Crafts and Businesses

- **Why**: Senegal is rich in artisanship, from woven fabrics to carved masks. Supporting local markets like Sandaga Market in Dakar ensures economic empowerment.
- **Where**:
  - o **Sandaga Market**
    - **Address**: Boulevard de la République, Dakar.
    - **Opening Hours**: Daily, 8:00 AM - 7:00 PM.
    - **Pricing**: Bargain expected; initial prices often 30-50% higher.

Don'ts in Senegalese Culture

1. Avoid Eating or Drinking in Public During Ramadan

- **Cultural Context**: During the holy month of Ramadan, most Senegalese Muslims fast from sunrise to sunset. Eating or drinking publicly can be seen as disrespectful.

- **What to Do Instead**: If you're not fasting, eat discreetly or within private accommodations.

2. Don't Point with Your Finger

- **Cultural Context**: Pointing directly with one finger is considered rude in Senegal.
- **What to Do**: Use your whole hand or gesture subtly.

3. Avoid Excessive Displays of Affection

- **Cultural Context**: Senegalese culture values modesty, and overt public displays of affection can make others uncomfortable.
- **What to Avoid**: Hand-holding is generally fine, but kissing or hugging in public is frowned upon, especially in conservative areas.

4. Don't Rush Conversations or Transactions

- **Cultural Context**: Senegalese culture emphasizes building relationships over hurried exchanges.
- **What to Do**: Engage in small talk before getting to the point. In markets, bargaining should be good-natured, not aggressive.

5. Avoid Criticizing Senegal's History or Religion

- **Cultural Context**: Religion and history are sources of pride. Criticism can be taken as a personal offense.
- **What to Do**: Approach sensitive topics with curiosity and respect.

2.6. Currency, Banking, and Mobile Connectivity

1. Currency Basics

- **Currency Name**: West African CFA Franc (XOF).
- **Symbol**: CFA or simply "F".

- **Exchange Rate**: Approximately 1 EUR = 655 XOF (fixed exchange rate). Rates for USD and other currencies fluctuate, so check current rates before exchanging.

2. Currency Denominations

- **Banknotes**: 500, 1,000, 2,000, 5,000, and 10,000 CFA Francs.
- **Coins**: 1, 5, 10, 25, 50, 100, 200, and 500 CFA Francs.

Banknotes are widely used, but coins are essential for small purchases such as street food, tipping, and local transport. Always carry smaller denominations, as vendors may lack change for larger notes.

3. Currency Exchange

- **Where to Exchange**:
  - **Banks**:
    - Example: **Ecobank Dakar**
      - **Address**: 5 Avenue Léopold Sédar Senghor, Dakar.
      - **Opening Hours**: Mon-Fri, 8:00 AM - 4:30 PM.
      - **Exchange Fees**: Typically 2-3% of the transaction amount.
  - **Bureau de Change**: Found at airports, major cities, and tourist areas.
    - Competitive rates, though they may charge higher fees.
  - **Hotels**: Offer currency exchange but often at less favorable rates.
- **Tips for Currency Exchange**:
  - Always count your money before leaving the counter.
  - Avoid exchanging money with unofficial street dealers.

Banking in Senegal

1. Major Banks and Services

Senegal has a robust banking system, with major players providing reliable services for locals and tourists alike.

- **Banks**:
    - ○ **Bank of Africa (BOA)**: Extensive ATM network across the country.
    - ○ **Société Générale Senegal**: Offers foreign currency withdrawals at select ATMs.
    - ○ **BNP Paribas Senegal**: Known for excellent customer service and English-speaking staff.
- **Banking Hours**:
    - ○ Monday to Friday: 8:00 AM - 4:00 PM.
    - ○ Closed on weekends and public holidays.

2. ATMs

ATMs are the most convenient way to access cash in Senegal. However, there are key considerations:

- **ATM Availability**:
    - ○ Widely available in major cities such as Dakar, Saint-Louis, and Ziguinchor.
    - ○ Scarce in rural areas, so stock up on cash before traveling outside urban centers.
- **Accepted Cards**:
    - ○ VISA is the most widely accepted card. Mastercard and Maestro are less common but available at certain banks.
- **ATM Fees**:

- International withdrawal fees typically range from XOF 2,000 to XOF 5,000 per transaction, depending on your bank.
    - Daily withdrawal limits vary, often capped at XOF 200,000.
- **Tips for Using ATMs**:
    - Use ATMs attached to banks for added security.
    - Withdraw larger amounts to minimize fees, but ensure safety when carrying cash.

3. Traveler's Checks and Cards

Traveler's checks are not widely accepted in Senegal and may involve high processing fees. Credit and debit cards are better options for larger transactions, such as hotel bookings and dining at upscale restaurants.

- **Popular Cards**: VISA and Mastercard are the most accepted. American Express is less common.
- **Where Cards Are Accepted**:
    - High-end hotels, restaurants, and supermarkets in cities.
    - Small vendors and rural establishments often operate on a cash-only basis.

Mobile Connectivity in Senegal

1. Mobile Networks

Senegal boasts a well-established mobile network system with several operators providing affordable and reliable services.

- **Major Providers**:

- **Orange Senegal**: The largest and most reliable network, offering excellent coverage across urban and rural areas.
- **Free Senegal**: Competitive pricing for data-heavy users.
- **Expresso Senegal**: Affordable packages but limited coverage in remote areas.

2. Getting a SIM Card

Purchasing a local SIM card is the best way to stay connected and save on international roaming charges.

- **Where to Buy**:
  - Authorized shops of Orange, Free, or Expresso.
  - Street vendors (ensure the SIM is new and sealed).
- **Requirements**:
  - A valid passport is usually required for registration.
- **Cost**:
  - SIM Card: XOF 1,000 - XOF 2,000.
  - Prepaid Data Plans: Start at XOF 500 for 1GB of data (valid for one day) to XOF 10,000 for 30GB (valid for one month).

3. Internet and Data

- **4G Coverage**: Available in cities and tourist hubs.
- **Wi-Fi**: Found in hotels, cafes, and restaurants in urban areas but often slow.
- **Data Speeds**: Reliable for basic browsing, social media, and video streaming, though speeds may drop in remote areas.

4. Useful Mobile Apps

- **Transportation**:

- o **Heetch**: Popular ride-hailing app in Dakar.

- **Navigation**:
  - o **Google Maps** and **Maps.me** work well for urban and rural navigation.

- **Language**:
  - o **Google Translate** or **SayHi Translate** for French and Wolof.

Practical Tips for Managing Money and Staying Connected

1. **Always Carry Cash**: Rural areas and small vendors rely exclusively on cash.

2. **Download Offline Maps**: Mobile coverage can be spotty in remote areas.

3. **Beware of Scams**: Only use official ATMs and authorized vendors.

4. **Secure Your Devices**: Use a VPN when accessing Wi-Fi to protect sensitive information.

CHAPTER 3

GETTING AROUND SENEGAL

Traveling through Senegal offers a mix of modern and traditional modes of transportation that cater to various preferences, budgets, and destinations. Whether you're flying between cities, taking a scenic train ride, or navigating rural roads by car, understanding the nuances of Senegal's transportation system is key to a smooth journey

Transportation Options

Planes: Domestic Flights in Senegal

For long-distance travel or reaching remote areas like Casamance, domestic flights are the most efficient option. Senegal has a reliable air transport network operated by key airlines.

1. Major Airports

- **Blaise Diagne International Airport (DSS)**
  - **Address**: Ndiass, 43 km from Dakar.
  - **Opening Hours**: 24/7.
  - **Facilities**: Restaurants, lounges, ATMs, and car rental services.
  - **Domestic Connections**: DSS serves as the primary hub for domestic flights to destinations such as Ziguinchor, Cap Skirring, and Tambacounda.
- **Ziguinchor Airport (ZIG)**

- o **Address**: Ziguinchor, Casamance region.
- o **Opening Hours**: 7:00 AM - 8:00 PM.
- o **Facilities**: Basic amenities and taxis available for onward travel.

2. Airlines and Routes

- **Air Senegal**
  - o **Routes**: Connects Dakar with Ziguinchor, Cap Skirring, and Tambacounda.
  - o **Pricing**: Starting at XOF 45,000 one-way.
  - o **Booking**: Online or at airport ticket counters.
- **Transair Senegal**
  - o **Routes**: Regional routes, including Dakar to Ziguinchor and Kolda.
  - o **Pricing**: Competitive rates starting at XOF 35,000.

3. Tips for Domestic Flights

- Book flights in advance during peak travel seasons (November–March).
- Arrive at the airport at least 90 minutes before domestic departures.
- Check luggage weight restrictions, as smaller aircraft may have stricter limits.

Trains: The Dakar-Bamako Railway

While trains in Senegal are limited in scope, they offer a unique and nostalgic way to experience the country's landscapes.

1. Overview of the Railway System

- **Route**: The Dakar-Bamako railway historically connected Dakar to Mali's capital, Bamako. However, full passenger services are not currently operational.
- **Regional Routes**: Limited short-haul train services operate between Dakar and nearby areas.

2. Tourist Train Experiences

Although regular train services are sparse, special tourist trains occasionally operate for cultural or scenic journeys. These experiences often showcase Senegal's stunning landscapes and rich heritage.

- **Example**: Historical train rides in Saint-Louis during cultural festivals.
- **Pricing**: XOF 10,000–XOF 20,000, depending on the event and route.

3. Future Developments

Senegal's government has announced plans to revitalize the railway network, including new routes and modern trains, with the goal of improving connectivity and tourism.

Automobiles: Roads and Vehicles in Senegal

Driving is the most flexible way to explore Senegal, especially for reaching off-the-beaten-path destinations. Roads vary in condition, from well-maintained highways to rugged rural tracks.

1. Renting a Car

Car rentals are available in major cities and airports. They are ideal for independent travelers who value flexibility.

- **Recommended Providers**:
  - **Avis Senegal**

- **Address**: Blaise Diagne International Airport and Dakar city center.
- **Opening Hours**: 7:00 AM - 10:00 PM.
- **Pricing**: Starting at XOF 35,000 per day for compact cars.

- **Europcar Senegal**
  - **Address**: Various locations in Dakar.
  - **Pricing**: From XOF 40,000 per day.

- **Vehicle Options**:
  - Sedans for city travel.
  - SUVs or 4x4 vehicles for rural areas and national parks.

- **Driving Requirements**:
  - International Driver's Permit (IDP) is recommended.
  - Minimum age: 21–25, depending on the rental company.

2. Taxis and Ride-Hailing Services

- **Taxis**:
  - Widely available in cities. Prices are negotiable, with short rides in Dakar costing around XOF 1,000–XOF 3,000.
  - Ensure to agree on the fare before starting your journey.

- **Ride-Hailing Apps**:
  - **Heetch**: Available in Dakar, offering competitive pricing and convenience.

3. Public Buses and Minibuses

- **Urban Buses**:

- o Operated by Dakar Dem Dikk in Dakar.
- o Fares: XOF 150–XOF 500, depending on the route.
- **Minibuses (Ndiaga Ndiaye)**:
  - o These iconic white minibuses connect cities and towns.
  - o Fares: Typically XOF 500–XOF 2,500 based on distance.

4. Intercity Travel

- **Sept-Place Taxis**: Shared station wagons that connect major cities.
  - o Capacity: Seven passengers.
  - o Pricing: XOF 5,000–XOF 10,000 per person for trips such as Dakar to Saint-Louis.
  - o Pros: Faster than buses.
  - o Cons: Can be cramped and uncomfortable.
- **Private Car Services**: Available for long-distance trips, offering comfort and flexibility at higher prices.

Road Safety and Driving Tips

1. **Road Conditions**:
   - o Highways between major cities are generally paved and in good condition.
   - o Rural roads may be unpaved and require a 4x4 vehicle.
2. **Navigation**:
   - o Use offline maps such as **Maps.me** in areas with poor mobile coverage.
   - o Roads are often poorly signposted, so double-check your route.
3. **Driving Rules**:

- Drive on the right-hand side of the road.
- Seat belts are mandatory.
- Avoid driving at night due to poor lighting and potential hazards.

4. **Fuel Availability**:
- Fuel stations are common in cities but sparse in rural areas. Carry extra fuel for long trips.

Unique Transport Experiences in Senegal

1. **Horse-Drawn Carts**
   - A traditional mode of transport in rural areas and small towns, offering a glimpse into local life.

2. **Pirogues (Traditional Boats)**
   - Used for river crossings and exploring coastal areas.
   - Example: Pirogue tours in the Sine-Saloum Delta.
   - Pricing: Starting at XOF 5,000 per person for guided trips.

Tips for Getting Around Senegal

1. Plan intercity travel during daylight hours to maximize safety.
2. Carry small denominations of cash for taxis, buses, and tolls.
3. If renting a car, familiarize yourself with local driving customs and traffic regulations.
4. Be prepared for delays, especially when using public transport.

Domestic Flights and Ferries

Domestic Flights in Senegal

Senegal's domestic aviation network is relatively well-developed, making air travel a practical option for covering long distances or reaching remote destinations like the Casamance region.

Key Domestic Airports

1. **Blaise Diagne International Airport (DSS)**
   - o **Location**: 43 km southeast of Dakar.
   - o **Facilities**: Cafes, duty-free shops, car rentals, currency exchange.
   - o **Connections**: Hub for domestic flights to Ziguinchor, Cap Skirring, and Tambacounda.

2. **Ziguinchor Airport (ZIG)**
   - o **Location**: Southern Senegal, gateway to the Casamance region.
   - o **Facilities**: Small terminal with basic amenities.

3. **Cap Skirring Airport (CSK)**
   - o **Location**: Popular coastal town in the Casamance.
   - o **Connections**: Seasonal flights to Dakar and nearby regional hubs.

4. **Saint-Louis Airport (XLS)**
   - o **Location**: Northern Senegal, serving the historic city of Saint-Louis.
   - o **Usage**: Primarily charter and private flights.

5. **Tambacounda Airport (TUD)**
   - o **Location**: Southeastern Senegal, ideal for accessing Niokolo-Koba National Park.

- Connections: Flights from Dakar operate occasionally.

Airlines Operating Domestic Flights

1. **Air Senegal**

   - **Hub**: Blaise Diagne International Airport.
   - **Routes**: Connects Dakar with Ziguinchor, Cap Skirring, and other regional destinations.
   - **Ticket Prices**:
     - Dakar to Ziguinchor: Approx. XOF 45,000–70,000 one-way.
     - Dakar to Cap Skirring: Approx. XOF 50,000–80,000 one-way.
   - **Booking Options**: Online via the official website, travel agents, or airport counters.

2. **Transair**

   - **Routes**: Offers additional connections to secondary airports like Tambacounda.
   - **Pricing**: Similar to Air Senegal.

Flight Schedules and Timing

- Domestic flights operate regularly but may be less frequent than in other countries.
- Always arrive at the airport at least 1.5 hours before departure for domestic flights.

Tips for Domestic Air Travel

1. **Plan Ahead**: Book flights early, especially during the high season (November to April).

2. **Luggage Restrictions**: Most airlines have a 20 kg checked luggage limit. Confirm baggage policies when booking.

3. **Check-In Locations**: Smaller airports may have limited services, so reconfirm your flight and arrive early.

4. **Accessibility**: Domestic airports often lack modern facilities, so prepare for basic services in regional hubs.

Ferries in Senegal

Ferries are an integral part of Senegal's transport system, particularly for accessing the Casamance region and island destinations like Gorée Island.

Key Ferry Routes and Services

1. **Dakar to Gorée Island**

   o **Operator**: Dakar Dem Dikk.

   o **Ferry Terminal**: Port of Dakar, located near Place de l'Indépendance.

   o **Schedule**:

     ▪ Weekdays: First departure at 7:00 AM; last return at 6:00 PM.

     ▪ Weekends: First departure at 8:00 AM; last return at 7:00 PM.

   o **Pricing**:

     ▪ Adults: XOF 5,200 round trip.

     ▪ Children: XOF 2,500 round trip.

   o **Journey Time**: 20–30 minutes.

   o **Details**: Ferries are reliable and offer stunning views of Dakar's coastline.

2. **Dakar to Ziguinchor (Casamance)**

   o **Operator**: L'Express du Sénégal.

- Ferry Terminal: Port of Dakar.
- Schedule: Twice weekly departures.
  - Departures: Tuesdays and Fridays at 8:00 PM.
  - Arrivals in Ziguinchor: Following morning at 10:00 AM.
- Pricing:
  - Economy Class: XOF 15,000.
  - First Class: XOF 35,000 (air-conditioned cabins).
  - Vehicle Transport: XOF 60,000–80,000 per vehicle.
- Journey Time: Approx. 14 hours.
- Details: This overnight ferry provides a comfortable way to reach the Casamance region. Onboard amenities include sleeping cabins, dining areas, and restrooms.

3. **Inter-Island Ferries (Sine-Saloum Delta)**
- Operators: Local private boats and pirogues.
- Popular Routes:
  - Djiffer to Foundiougne.
  - Saloum Islands for eco-tourism.
- Pricing: XOF 1,000–5,000, depending on the route.
- Details: These smaller ferries are less formal but provide scenic views of mangroves and waterways.

Ferry Facilities

- **Onboard Services**: Larger ferries like the Dakar-Ziguinchor route offer cabins, food, and beverages. Smaller ferries are basic, with limited seating.
- **Safety**: Life jackets are usually available, but it's advisable to carry your own for smaller ferries.

Tips for Ferry Travel

1. **Book in Advance**: Ferries, especially on the Dakar-Ziguinchor route, can fill up quickly.
2. **Arrive Early**: Arrive at least an hour before departure to secure seating and handle ticketing formalities.
3. **Pack Essentials**: Bring snacks, water, and entertainment for longer journeys.
4. **Weather Considerations**: Ferry schedules may be disrupted during the rainy season (June to October).

Dining and Accommodation Near Ferry Terminals and Airports

Dining Options

1. **Dakar Port Area**
   - **Le Lagon 1**:
     - **Address**: Route de la Corniche Est, Dakar.
     - **Cuisine**: Seafood with ocean views.
     - **Pricing**: XOF 15,000–30,000 per person.
2. **Ziguinchor Port Area**
   - **Restaurant Le Kassa**:
     - **Cuisine**: Traditional Senegalese dishes.
     - **Pricing**: XOF 7,000–15,000.

Accommodation Options

1. **Near Blaise Diagne International Airport**
   o **Radisson Hotel Dakar Diamniadio**:
     ▪ **Pricing**: XOF 120,000 per night.
     ▪ **Facilities**: Pool, Wi-Fi, airport shuttle.
2. **Near Ziguinchor Ferry Terminal**
   o **Hotel Kadiandoumagne**:
     ▪ **Pricing**: XOF 50,000–80,000 per night.
     ▪ **Facilities**: Riverside views, traditional decor.

Public Transportation: Buses, Taxis, and Car Rentals

1. Public Transportation Modes in Senegal

Dakar Dem Dikk (Public Buses)

Dakar Dem Dikk is the state-owned bus company operating within Dakar and its suburbs, as well as intercity routes across Senegal.

- **Address**: Main terminal at Petersen Station, Rue Moussé Diop, Dakar.
- **Opening Hours**: Daily, 5:00 AM – 10:00 PM.
- **Pricing**:
  o Urban routes: XOF 150–500 per trip.
  o Intercity routes: XOF 5,000–20,000, depending on distance.

Features:

- Comfortable, affordable, and reasonably punctual within Dakar.
- Air-conditioned buses operate on some intercity routes.

Tips:

- Carry small denominations of cash for ticket purchases.
- Arrive early for intercity buses, as seats fill quickly.

Ndiaga Ndiaye (Shared Minibuses)

Ndiaga Ndiaye minibuses are ubiquitous across Senegal, offering a quintessential local experience.

- **Availability**: Found at major bus stations and street corners.
- **Pricing**: XOF 100–300 for short urban trips; XOF 1,500–7,000 for intercity travel.

Features:

- Typically 14–30-seater vehicles painted white with colorful designs.
- Operates on fixed routes but stops frequently to pick up and drop off passengers.

Pros:

- Extremely affordable.
- Available even in remote areas.

Cons:

- Crowded and often delayed.
- Older vehicles may lack comfort and safety features.

Tips:

- Expect to share space with other passengers, and pack light as luggage space is limited.
- Be patient, as these buses wait until full before departing.

Car Rapides (Colorful Minibuses)

Car Rapides are iconic symbols of Senegalese public transport, particularly in Dakar.

- **Availability**: Operates extensively in Dakar and surrounding suburbs.
- **Pricing**: XOF 50–300 depending on the distance.

Features:

- Brightly painted minibuses with open doors and a driver's assistant shouting out destinations.
- Stops anywhere along its route, making it a flexible option.

Pros:

- A budget-friendly way to navigate urban areas.
- Provides a glimpse into everyday Senegalese life.

Cons:

- Often overcrowded, with passengers standing.
- No fixed schedules; departure times depend on passenger demand.

Tips:

- Confirm the destination with the assistant before boarding.
- Keep your valuables secure, as pickpocketing can occur in crowded spaces.

---

2. Intercity Travel in Senegal

Sept-Place Taxis (Shared Long-Distance Taxis)

Sept-place taxis are station wagons converted into shared taxis for intercity travel.

- **Address**: Found at major taxi ranks like Gare Routière de Pompiers in Dakar.
- **Opening Hours**: Depart as soon as all seats are filled, typically between 5:00 AM and 7:00 PM.
- **Pricing**: XOF 5,000–15,000 depending on the route.

Features:
- Accommodates seven passengers plus a driver.
- Faster than buses due to fewer stops.

Pros:
- Efficient for medium-distance travel.
- Available even in rural areas.

Cons:
- Limited comfort due to overcrowding.
- Vehicles may not meet high safety standards.

Tips:
- Pay extra to reserve an additional seat for more space.
- Inspect the vehicle condition and negotiate prices before boarding.

Intercity Buses

Private bus companies complement Dakar Dem Dikk's intercity service.

- **Examples**:
  - **Ndiaga Ndiaye Grand Luxe**: Offers more comfort than standard Ndiaga Ndiaye minibuses.
  - **Senbus**: Known for reliable service.
- **Pricing**: XOF 5,000–25,000 depending on distance and class.

Features:

- Options for regular and luxury buses.
- Amenities such as air conditioning and reclining seats on premium services.

Tips:

- Book tickets in advance during peak travel seasons.
- Carry snacks and water for long trips, as breaks can be infrequent.

Trains

Senegal's rail system is undergoing revitalization, but currently, the Dakar–Blaise Diagne International Airport (DSS) Express Train is the standout option.

- **Address**: Main station in Dakar at Gare de Dakar.
- **Opening Hours**: Daily, 6:00 AM – 11:00 PM.
- **Pricing**: XOF 2,500 for standard class, XOF 5,000 for first class.

Features:

- Connects Dakar to DSS and Diamniadio.
- Comfortable seating, air conditioning, and reliable schedules.

Pros:

- Avoids road traffic congestion.
- Safe and efficient.

Tips:

- Arrive 30 minutes before departure for security checks.
- Tickets can be purchased online or at the station.

---

3. Urban Transport Options

Taxis

Yellow taxis are available throughout Senegal's cities and towns.

- **Pricing**: Fares range from XOF 1,000–3,000 within cities.
- **Features**:
    - No meters; negotiate fare upfront.
    - Air conditioning is rare.

Tips:

- Use smaller bills for payment.
- Insist on a fair price if the initial quote seems high.

Motorcycle Taxis (Jakarta)

Jakarta motorcycle taxis are common in smaller towns and rural areas.

- **Pricing**: XOF 100–1,000 depending on the distance.

Pros:

- Quick and efficient for short distances.
- Can navigate traffic jams.

Cons:

- Less safe than other options. Helmets are rarely provided.

Ride-Hailing Apps

- **Heetch**: Available in Dakar, offering an alternative to traditional taxis.
    - **Pricing**: XOF 1,500–3,500 for most city trips.

Features:

- Fixed pricing via the app.

- Secure and convenient for tourists.

Tips:

- Download the app before arrival and set up payment options.

---

4. Navigating Public Transport

Communication

Most drivers and assistants speak French and Wolof. Basic phrases such as "Combien?" (How much?) and "Je veux aller à..." (I want to go to...) can be helpful.

Luggage Considerations

- Larger vehicles like buses and sept-place taxis offer limited luggage space.
- Pack compactly, especially for Ndiaga Ndiaye and Car Rapides.

Timing and Patience

Public transport in Senegal operates on flexible schedules, so patience is essential. Allow extra time for delays, especially when transferring between modes.

---

5. Costs and Budgeting

Public transport in Senegal is incredibly affordable, with options catering to every budget. Travelers can spend as little as XOF 50 on a Car Rapide or invest in a comfortable intercity bus ride for XOF 15,000.

Navigating Senegal's Roads

1. Senegal's Road Network Overview

Primary Roads

Senegal boasts several well-maintained highways connecting major cities and regions:

- **N1 (National Highway 1)**: Links Dakar to the southeastern city of Tambacounda and beyond.
- **N2**: Runs through the northern regions, connecting Saint-Louis to Matam.
- **N4**: Covers the southern Casamance region, connecting Ziguinchor to Kolda.

Secondary and Rural Roads

Secondary roads are less maintained, and many rural paths are unpaved. Travelers venturing into remote areas should expect dirt tracks that may require a 4x4 vehicle, especially during the rainy season (June to October).

---

2. Self-Driving in Senegal

Self-driving provides the most flexibility for exploring Senegal's varied terrain. However, it requires careful planning and an understanding of local conditions.

Car Rentals

- **Where to Rent**:
  - **Europcar Senegal**
    - **Address**: Blaise Diagne International Airport (DSS), Dakar.
    - **Opening Hours**: 24/7.
    - **Pricing**: From XOF 40,000 per day for a standard car; XOF 70,000+ for a 4x4.
  - **Sahara Auto Rentals**
    - **Address**: Rue Carnot, Dakar.
    - **Opening Hours**: Mon-Sat, 8:00 AM - 6:00 PM.
    - **Pricing**: Negotiable, starting at XOF 35,000 per day.

- **Requirements**:
  - ○ Valid international driver's license.
  - ○ Minimum driving age: 21 years.

Fuel Stations

- Fuel is widely available in cities and along highways but can be scarce in rural areas. Major fuel companies include Total, Shell, and Elton.
- **Cost**: XOF 890 - XOF 1,100 per liter (diesel or gasoline).

Driving Conditions

- Roads in urban areas and major highways are paved and generally in good condition.
- Rural roads can be narrow, bumpy, and poorly marked.
- **Rainy Season Challenges**: Flooded roads and muddy tracks are common; a 4x4 is essential during this period.

Traffic Rules

- Drive on the right-hand side.
- Seat belts are mandatory for all passengers.
- Speed limits:
  - ○ Urban areas: 50 km/h.
  - ○ Highways: 90 km/h (unless otherwise posted).
- Carry all necessary documents, including vehicle registration, insurance, and your driver's license.

---

3. Public Transport Options

For those not comfortable driving, Senegal offers a variety of public transportation modes.

Taxis

- **Urban Taxis**:

- Widely available in cities like Dakar and Saint-Louis.
- No meters; fares must be negotiated in advance.
- Typical fares: XOF 1,500 - XOF 3,500 for short trips in Dakar.

- **Shared Taxis**:
  - Known as "clandos" in local slang.
  - Operate along fixed routes and are cheaper but less comfortable.

Buses and Minibuses

- **Ndiaga Ndiaye Minibuses**:
  - Popular for intercity travel.
  - No fixed schedules; buses depart when full.
  - Fares: XOF 500 - XOF 3,000, depending on distance.
- **Public Buses**:
  - Operate within cities and are the most affordable option.
  - Fares: Starting at XOF 100 per ride.

Sept-Places (Seven-Seaters)

- These shared station wagons connect towns and regions.
- Faster than buses but less spacious.
- Fares: XOF 2,000 - XOF 8,000, depending on distance.

Ferries

- Essential for travel to regions like Casamance.
  - Example: **Dakar-Ziguinchor Ferry**
    - **Departure Location**: Port of Dakar.
    - **Schedule**: Twice weekly (Tuesday and Friday).
    - **Pricing**: Economy class: XOF 10,000; Cabin: XOF 25,000.

4. Navigating Dakar's Traffic

Dakar's roads are notoriously congested, especially during peak hours (7:00 AM - 9:00 AM and 5:00 PM - 7:00 PM).

Tips for Navigating Dakar

- Use ride-hailing apps like **Heetch** for reliable and reasonably priced transport.
- Avoid driving in downtown Dakar unless necessary; parking is scarce.
- Be prepared for chaotic traffic and assertive driving styles.

Pedestrian Navigation

Sidewalks are not always available, so pedestrians share roads with vehicles. Exercise caution when walking in busy areas.

5. Travel to Remote Areas

Road Conditions

- Unpaved roads dominate rural Senegal.
- During the rainy season, some roads become impassable due to flooding.

Recommended Vehicles

- Rent a 4x4 for remote areas or join guided tours with reliable transport.

Villages and Natural Reserves

- **Niokolo-Koba National Park**
  - **Address**: Near Tambacounda, southeastern Senegal.
  - **Access**: Via N7; dirt roads lead to park entrances.
  - **Road Challenges**: Rough terrain; 4x4 recommended.
- **Sine-Saloum Delta**

- o **Access**: Reachable via N1 and secondary roads.

---

6. Safety and Practical Advice

Safety Tips

- Avoid traveling at night due to poor road lighting and the risk of accidents.
- Watch out for livestock crossing roads, especially in rural areas.
- Always lock car doors and avoid leaving valuables visible.

Emergency Contacts

- Police: 17
- Road Assistance: **Total Senegal** offers roadside help (call details at stations).

---

7. Cost of Traveling by Road

Sample Costs

- Taxi from Blaise Diagne International Airport to Dakar: XOF 20,000 - XOF 25,000.
- Bus from Dakar to Saint-Louis: XOF 4,000.
- Renting a 4x4 for a week: XOF 250,000 - XOF 350,000.

CHAPTER.4.

TOP DESTINATIONS IN SENEGAL

Dakar: The Vibrant Capital City

Dakar, Senegal's vibrant capital, is the beating heart of West Africa. A city that seamlessly blends traditional African culture with French colonial influences, Dakar offers a kaleidoscope of experiences for travelers. From historical landmarks and bustling markets to serene beaches and gourmet dining, this metropolis is a must-see destination for anyone visiting Senegal. Here's a detailed guide to discovering Dakar, complete with essential information for attractions, dining, and accommodations.

Historical and Cultural Landmarks

Gorée Island (Île de Gorée)

- **Address**: Accessible via ferry from Dakar Port.
- **Opening Hours**: Daily, 9:00 AM - 6:00 PM.
- **Pricing**: Ferry ticket: XOF 5,200 (round trip). Entrance to the House of Slaves: XOF 500.

This UNESCO World Heritage Site is a haunting reminder of the transatlantic slave trade. Key attractions on the island include:

- **House of Slaves (Maison des Esclaves)**: A poignant museum detailing the horrors of the slave trade.
- **Fort d'Estrées**: Now a museum showcasing Senegal's history and culture.
- **Art Galleries and Markets**: Local artists display vibrant works inspired by African heritage.

African Renaissance Monument

- **Address**: Route de la Corniche Ouest, Dakar.
- **Opening Hours**: Daily, 9:00 AM - 6:00 PM.
- **Pricing**: XOF 6,000 for entry and guided tour.

This 49-meter bronze statue, the tallest in Africa, symbolizes Africa's emergence from colonial rule. Visitors can climb to the top for panoramic views of Dakar. A small museum at the base provides insights into Senegalese history and culture.

Museum of Black Civilizations (Musée des Civilisations Noires)

- **Address**: Avenue Cheikh Anta Diop, Dakar.
- **Opening Hours**: Tue-Sun, 9:00 AM - 6:00 PM.
- **Pricing**: XOF 5,000 for adults; XOF 2,000 for students.

This modern museum celebrates the achievements of Black civilizations worldwide, with exhibits spanning ancient artifacts, contemporary art, and historical manuscripts.

Markets and Shopping

Sandaga Market

- **Address**: Rue Sandaga, Dakar.
- **Opening Hours**: Mon-Sat, 8:00 AM - 8:00 PM.
- **Tips**: Bargaining is essential to get the best prices.

A bustling market offering everything from vibrant textiles and handcrafted jewelry to spices and fresh produce. It's a sensory overload, perfect for those seeking an authentic African shopping experience.

Soumbédioune Craft Market

- **Address**: Corniche Ouest, Dakar.
- **Opening Hours**: Daily, 9:00 AM - 7:00 PM.

Specializing in artisan goods, this market is ideal for finding unique souvenirs such as carved wooden masks, woven baskets, and colorful paintings.

Beaches and Waterfront Attractions

Ngor Island (Île de Ngor)

- **Access**: Short pirogue (traditional boat) ride from Ngor Beach.
- **Pricing**: Boat ride: XOF 1,000. Beach access fee: XOF 500.

A tranquil escape from Dakar's hustle, Ngor Island offers golden sands, clear waters, and laid-back beach bars. Activities include swimming, kayaking, and enjoying fresh seafood.

Plage de Virage

- **Location**: Near Dakar's airport.
- **Activities**: Surfing, kiteboarding, and beachside dining.
- **Pricing**: Free entry; equipment rental starts at XOF 10,000.

This popular beach attracts both locals and tourists. Surfing lessons are available for beginners.

Dining in Dakar

Fine Dining

- **La Maison Blanche**
  - ○ **Address**: Almadies Road, Dakar.
  - ○ **Cuisine**: French-Senegalese fusion.
  - ○ **Average Cost**: XOF 15,000 - XOF 25,000 per person.
- **Le Lagon 1**
  - ○ **Address**: Route de la Corniche Est, Dakar.
  - ○ **Cuisine**: Seafood, featuring lobster and oysters.
  - ○ **Average Cost**: XOF 20,000 per person.

Local Eateries

- **Chez Loutcha**
  - ○ **Address**: Rue Mousse Diop, Dakar.
  - ○ **Cuisine**: Authentic Senegalese dishes like *thieboudienne* and *yassa*.
  - ○ **Average Cost**: XOF 5,000 per meal.
- **Soumbedioune Night Market**
  - ○ Enjoy freshly grilled fish and local street food while soaking in the lively atmosphere.

Accommodation in Dakar

Luxury Hotels

- **Radisson Blu Hotel Dakar Sea Plaza**
  - ○ **Address**: Route de la Corniche Ouest.
  - ○ **Pricing**: From XOF 90,000 per night.

- - **Amenities**: Ocean-view rooms, infinity pool, spa, and fine dining.
- **Terrou-Bi Resort**
  - **Address**: Boulevard Martin Luther King, Dakar.
  - **Pricing**: From XOF 100,000 per night.
  - **Highlights**: Private beach, casino, and upscale dining.

Mid-Range Options

- **Onomo Hotel Dakar Airport**
  - **Address**: Route de Ngor, Dakar.
  - **Pricing**: From XOF 45,000 per night.
- **Café de Rome**
  - **Address**: Plateau, Dakar.
  - **Pricing**: From XOF 35,000 per night.

Budget Accommodations

- **Auberge Keur Diame**
  - **Address**: Yoff, Dakar.
  - **Pricing**: From XOF 10,000 per night.

Nightlife and Entertainment

Théâtre National Daniel Sorano

- **Address**: Boulevard de la République, Dakar.
- **Opening Hours**: Performance schedules vary; evening shows start at 8:00 PM.
- **Pricing**: XOF 2,000 - XOF 10,000 depending on the event.

This theater hosts a range of performances, including traditional Senegalese dance, live music, and plays.

Almadies Nightclubs

The Almadies district is the hub for Dakar's nightlife. Popular spots include:

- **Le Vogue**: Known for its international DJs and vibrant dance floor.
- **Le Patio**: A relaxed lounge with live jazz and cocktails.

---

7. Practical Tips for Exploring Dakar

1. **Transport**:
   - Use ride-hailing apps like Heetch for reliable transport within the city.
   - Taxis are plentiful but require negotiation.
2. **Language**: French is widely spoken, but learning basic Wolof phrases will enhance your interactions.
3. **Safety**:
   - Stay alert in crowded areas to avoid pickpocketing.
   - Avoid walking alone at night in less busy neighborhoods.
4. **Best Time to Visit**:
   - The dry season (November to May) offers pleasant weather for outdoor activities.

Saint-Louis: The Colonial Gem

Saint-Louis, located in northern Senegal, is a vibrant city steeped in history and culture. Known as the former capital of French West Africa, this UNESCO World Heritage Site combines colonial charm, vibrant arts, and breathtaking natural beauty. From its picturesque architecture to its serene beaches and nature reserves, Saint-Louis is a must-visit for every traveler exploring Senegal. This guide dives deep into what Saint-Louis offers, ensuring you have the best insights for your visit.

Getting to Saint-Louis

By Road

- **From Dakar**:
    - **Distance**: Approximately 270 kilometers (4-5 hours by car).
    - **Route**: N1 and N2 highways.
    - **Transportation Options**:
        - **Private Car**: Rent from Dakar for approximately XOF 40,000 per day.
        - **Sept-Places (shared taxis)**: Cost around XOF 5,000 per seat.
        - **Intercity Buses**: Starting at XOF 4,000.

By Air

- Saint-Louis Airport is currently not operational for commercial flights. Most travelers arrive via Blaise Diagne International Airport in Dakar and then continue by road.

Top Attractions in Saint-Louis

1. Faidherbe Bridge

- **Address**: Connecting the mainland to the island of Saint-Louis.
- **Opening Hours**: Open 24/7.
- **Pricing**: Free access for pedestrians and vehicles.

The Faidherbe Bridge, an iconic symbol of Saint-Louis, was designed by Gustave Eiffel's engineering team. Spanning the Senegal River, it offers stunning views of the city and riverbanks, especially at sunrise and sunset. Strolling across the bridge is a quintessential experience, offering insight into the city's colonial heritage.

---

2. The Island of Saint-Louis (Ndar)

- **Address**: Central Saint-Louis.
- **Opening Hours**: Always accessible.
- **Pricing**: Free to explore; guided tours start at XOF 5,000 per person.

This island is the historical heart of Saint-Louis, characterized by narrow streets, brightly colored colonial buildings, and a lively atmosphere. Key highlights include:

- **Governor's Palace**: A colonial-era structure that showcases Saint-Louis' administrative legacy.
- **The Cathedral of Saint-Louis**: Built in 1828, it's one of West Africa's oldest Catholic churches.
- **Local Markets**: Bustling with vendors selling crafts, spices, and fabrics.

---

3. Langue de Barbarie National Park

- **Address**: 18 kilometers south of Saint-Louis.
- **Opening Hours**: Daily, 8:00 AM – 6:00 PM.
- **Pricing**: Entry fee XOF 3,000 per person; boat tours start at XOF 15,000.

This coastal national park is a haven for birdwatchers, offering sightings of pelicans, flamingos, and other migratory birds. It's also home to pristine beaches and dunes, perfect for relaxation or eco-tourism.

---

4. Guet Ndar Fishing District

- **Address**: Northwestern Saint-Louis, near the Atlantic coast.
- **Opening Hours**: Best visited early morning or late afternoon.
- **Pricing**: Free to visit; guided tours cost XOF 2,500.

This vibrant fishing community offers a glimpse into local life. Colorful pirogues (traditional fishing boats) line the shore, and you can watch the fishermen bringing in their daily catch. The district's lively markets and street food stalls are a culinary delight.

5. Djoudj National Bird Sanctuary

- **Address**: 60 kilometers north of Saint-Louis.
- **Opening Hours**: Daily, 8:00 AM – 6:00 PM (seasonal; best visited November to April).
- **Pricing**: Entry fee XOF 5,000 per person; guided tours start at XOF 10,000.

One of the world's most important bird sanctuaries, Djoudj is home to over 400 bird species. Highlights include flamingos, pelicans, and herons. The serene boat rides through the wetlands are unforgettable.

Dining in Saint-Louis

1. Flamingo Restaurant

- **Address**: Quai Henry Jay, Saint-Louis.
- **Opening Hours**: Daily, 12:00 PM – 10:00 PM.
- **Pricing**: XOF 7,000 – XOF 15,000 per meal.

Located by the river, Flamingo serves fresh seafood, including grilled fish and prawns. The terrace offers beautiful views of the Faidherbe Bridge.

2. La Linguère

- **Address**: Rue Blaise Diagne, Saint-Louis.
- **Opening Hours**: Daily, 7:30 AM – 9:00 PM.
- **Pricing**: XOF 5,000 – XOF 12,000 per meal.

Known for its blend of Senegalese and French cuisine, La Linguère offers dishes like yassa poulet and beef bourguignon.

Accommodation in Saint-Louis

1. Hotel de La Poste

- **Address**: Avenue Jean Mermoz, Saint-Louis.
- **Pricing**: Rooms start at XOF 35,000 per night.
- **Highlights**: Colonial-style architecture, comfortable rooms, and proximity to the Faidherbe Bridge.

2. Lodge Ocean & Savane

- **Address**: Langue de Barbarie, south of Saint-Louis.
- **Pricing**: Rooms from XOF 50,000 per night.
- **Highlights**: Secluded beachfront location and eco-lodging options.

Festivals and Events in Saint-Louis

1. Saint-Louis Jazz Festival

- **When**: May (exact dates vary).
- **Location**: Multiple venues across the city.
- **Pricing**: Tickets range from XOF 5,000 to XOF 20,000 depending on the event.

This internationally renowned festival attracts top musicians from Africa and beyond. The vibrant atmosphere includes open-air concerts, workshops, and jam sessions.

Practical Tips for Visiting Saint-Louis

1. **Best Time to Visit**:
   - November to April for pleasant weather and birdwatching.
2. **Getting Around**:
   - Hire a guide or rent bicycles (XOF 2,000–5,000 per day) for exploring the island.
3. **Cultural Etiquette**:
   - Dress modestly and always ask permission before photographing locals.

Gorée Island: A UNESCO World Heritage Site

Gorée Island, or **Île de Gorée**, is one of Senegal's most significant historical and cultural landmarks. Located just off the coast of Dakar, it is a UNESCO World Heritage Site that bears witness to the harrowing history of the transatlantic slave trade. At the same time, it offers visitors serene beauty, a sense of resilience, and vibrant local culture. This guide provides in-depth details on visiting Gorée Island, including key attractions, dining, accommodation, and travel tips.

Essential Information

- **Address**: Gorée Island, off the coast of Dakar, Senegal.
- **Access**: By ferry from the Port of Dakar.

- **Ferry Schedule**:
  - Departures from Dakar: Every 1–2 hours between 7:00 AM and 11:00 PM.
  - Departures from Gorée Island: Similarly spaced throughout the day.
- **Ferry Pricing**:
  - Locals: XOF 1,500 round trip.
  - Foreigners: XOF 5,200 round trip.
  - Children: XOF 1,000.
- **Entry Fees**:
  - Adults: XOF 500 for general entry to the island.
  - Additional fees for museums and attractions (detailed below).
- **Best Time to Visit**:
  - November to May (dry season) for pleasant weather and minimal rain.

Historical and Cultural Attractions on Gorée Island

1. The House of Slaves (Maison des Esclaves)

- **Address**: Central Gorée Island.
- **Opening Hours**:
  - Monday to Saturday: 10:00 AM - 5:00 PM.
  - Sunday: Closed for maintenance.
- **Entry Fee**: XOF 500 per person.

The House of Slaves is the island's most iconic site, a poignant reminder of the transatlantic slave trade. Built in the late 18th century, it served as a holding facility for enslaved people before they were shipped to the Americas.

- **Key Features**:
  - **The Door of No Return**: A small, arched exit through which countless enslaved people walked, never to return.
  - **Living Quarters**: Small, cramped cells where enslaved individuals were kept.
  - **Museum Exhibits**: Artifacts, documents, and narratives that depict the horrors of slavery.
- **Tour Highlights**: Guided tours provide historical context and share stories of resilience and cultural preservation.

2. Gorée Castle (Fort d'Estrées)

- **Address**: Northern tip of the island.
- **Opening Hours**: Daily, 9:00 AM - 6:00 PM.
- **Entry Fee**: Included in the island entry ticket.

Originally built as a fort in the 19th century, it now houses a museum showcasing Senegal's colonial and military history.

- **Key Features**:
  - Exhibits on French colonial rule.
  - Artifacts from Senegalese resistance movements.
  - Stunning views of Dakar from the ramparts.

3. St. Charles Church

- **Address**: Central Gorée Island, near the main plaza.
- **Opening Hours**: Open daily for visitors and Sunday services.
- **Entry Fee**: Free (donations encouraged).

A historic Catholic church built in the 19th century, it remains an active place of worship and a symbol of the island's diverse religious history.

Art and Cultural Experiences

1. Artists' Village

Located near the main plaza, the village is a vibrant hub of local artistry.

- **Opening Hours**: Daily, 9:00 AM - 7:00 PM.
- **Offerings**:
    - Paintings, sculptures, and crafts by local artists.
    - Live art demonstrations.
    - Opportunities to purchase authentic Senegalese art.

2. Gorée Institute

- **Address**: Southern Gorée Island.
- **Opening Hours**: By appointment.
- **Entry Fee**: XOF 1,000 for events and workshops.

This cultural and educational institute organizes workshops, seminars, and performances focused on African art, culture, and history.

Beaches and Relaxation

While Gorée Island is most famous for its history, it also offers picturesque beaches perfect for unwinding.

1. Plage de Gorée (Gorée Beach)

- **Location**: Near the ferry terminal.
- **Activities**:
    - Swimming in calm, clear waters.
    - Snorkeling to explore marine life.

2. Hidden Coves

Smaller, quieter beaches are scattered around the island, ideal for travelers seeking solitude.

Dining Options on Gorée Island

1. Chez Tonton Restaurant

- **Address**: Near the main plaza.
- **Opening Hours**: 11:00 AM - 10:00 PM.
- **Specialties**: Grilled fish, yassa poulet (chicken yassa), and fresh juices.
- **Pricing**: Meals range from XOF 3,000 - XOF 8,000.

2. Café Gorée

- **Address**: Along the southern promenade.
- **Opening Hours**: 8:00 AM - 8:00 PM.
- **Specialties**: Light snacks, coffee, and local pastries.

3. L'Escale Gourmande

- **Address**: Near the House of Slaves.
- **Opening Hours**: 12:00 PM - 9:00 PM.
- **Specialties**: French-Senegalese fusion cuisine.

Accommodation on Gorée Island

For those wishing to stay overnight, Gorée Island offers a few boutique accommodations.

1. Maison Augustin Ly

- **Address**: Near the ferry terminal.
- **Pricing**: XOF 25,000 - XOF 40,000 per night.

- **Features**:
  - Colonial-style architecture.
  - Complimentary breakfast.

2. La Maison du Marin
- **Address**: Southern Gorée Island.
- **Pricing**: XOF 20,000 - XOF 30,000 per night.
- **Features**:
  - Cozy rooms with sea views.
  - On-site restaurant.

Casamance Region: Senegal's Tropical Paradise

The Casamance Region, located in southern Senegal, is a lush and culturally rich area that offers a stark contrast to the country's arid north. Known for its verdant landscapes, intricate waterways, and vibrant traditions, this region is a must-visit for those seeking an authentic and tranquil Senegalese experience. From exploring pristine beaches to immersing yourself in the unique Diola culture, here's an in-depth guide to uncovering the wonders of Casamance.

Getting to Casamance

By Air
- **Ziguinchor Airport**
  - **Address**: Route de l'Aéroport, Ziguinchor.
  - **Flights**: Daily flights from Dakar (Blaise Diagne International Airport).

- o **Pricing**: Approximately XOF 40,000–60,000 for a one-way ticket.
- o **Airlines**: Air Senegal and Transair operate regular routes.

By Ferry

- **Dakar-Ziguinchor Ferry**
  - o **Departure Location**: Port of Dakar.
  - o **Schedule**: Twice weekly (Tuesday and Friday).
  - o **Duration**: Approximately 16 hours.
  - o **Pricing**:
    - Economy Class: XOF 10,000.
    - Cabin: XOF 25,000–50,000 depending on class.
  - o **Facilities**: Onboard dining, air-conditioned cabins, and entertainment areas.

By Road

Driving to Casamance requires crossing The Gambia, so you'll need to plan for border formalities. Ensure your vehicle has the necessary documentation and consider taking the Banjul ferry for a shorter crossing.

Key Attractions in Casamance

1. Cap Skirring

A coastal paradise known for its white sandy beaches and laid-back vibe.

- **Address**: Cap Skirring, Oussouye Department.
- **Best Time to Visit**: November to April (dry season).
- **Entry Fee**: Free.

What to Do:

- Relax on **Plage de Cap Skirring**, one of Senegal's most picturesque beaches.
- Try water sports such as kayaking, jet skiing, and snorkeling.
- Visit the **Cap Skirring Craft Market** for handmade Diola baskets, textiles, and jewelry.

Dining:

- **Le Petit Zing**
  - **Cuisine**: Local and French fusion.
  - **Specialties**: Grilled prawns and Diola-style rice.
  - **Pricing**: Meals from XOF 8,000.

Accommodation:

- **Hotel Les Alizés Beach Resort**
  - **Address**: Cap Skirring Beach.
  - **Pricing**: XOF 80,000–150,000 per night.
  - **Facilities**: Ocean-view rooms, spa, pool, and private beach.

---

2. Ziguinchor

The capital of the region, Ziguinchor is the cultural and economic hub of Casamance.

- **Address**: Ziguinchor City Center.
- **Best Time to Visit**: Year-round.

What to Do:

- Explore the **Cathédrale Saint-Antoine-de-Padoue**, a stunning example of colonial architecture.

- Visit the **Ziguinchor Regional Museum** to learn about Diola culture and the region's history.
- Stroll along the **Casamance River**, offering serene views and local fishing scenes.

Dining:
- **Le Perroquet**
  - **Cuisine**: Senegalese and European dishes.
  - **Specialties**: Yassa poulet (chicken in lemon-onion sauce).
  - **Pricing**: Meals from XOF 6,000.

Accommodation:
- **Kadiandoumagne Hotel**
  - **Address**: Avenue Emile Badiane, Ziguinchor.
  - **Pricing**: XOF 50,000–90,000 per night.
  - **Facilities**: Riverside views, a swimming pool, and lush gardens.

---

3. Oussouye

A cultural heartland, Oussouye is the perfect place to connect with the Diola people and their traditions.
- **Address**: Oussouye Town, 40 km from Ziguinchor.
- **Entry Fee**: Free.

What to Do:
- Attend a **Diola festival**, showcasing traditional music, dance, and rituals.
- Visit the sacred **Fromager Tree**, considered a spiritual symbol in local beliefs.

- Explore nearby villages via bicycle to witness authentic rural life.

Dining:

- **Chez Fifi**
  - **Cuisine**: Local dishes with a focus on fresh ingredients.
  - **Specialties**: Palm wine and millet-based meals.
  - **Pricing**: Meals from XOF 4,000.

Accommodation:

- **Ecolodge de Palmarin**
  - **Address**: Palmarin-Oussouye Road.
  - **Pricing**: XOF 35,000–60,000 per night.
  - **Facilities**: Traditional huts, eco-friendly design, and village tours.

---

4. Kafountine

A fishing village that offers an off-the-beaten-path experience.

- **Address**: Kafountine, 80 km from Ziguinchor.
- **Entry Fee**: Free.

What to Do:

- Visit the bustling **Kafountine Fish Market**, where you can see freshly caught fish being smoked or dried.
- Take a boat tour of the nearby mangroves, home to diverse bird species.
- Enjoy local drumming and dance performances at community gatherings.

Dining:

- **La Paillote Gourmande**

- Cuisine: Senegalese and international dishes.
- Specialties: Grilled fish with local spices.
- Pricing: Meals from XOF 5,000.

Accommodation:

- **Chez Hélène Guesthouse**
  - **Address**: Central Kafountine.
  - **Pricing**: XOF 25,000–40,000 per night.
  - **Facilities**: Simple rooms, friendly hosts, and a garden.

Cultural Highlights

1. Traditional Diola Architecture

In villages like Mlomp, you'll find multi-storied earthen homes built by the Diola people. These structures showcase impressive craftsmanship and provide insights into local engineering techniques.

2. Diola Rituals and Festivals

The Diola people have a rich tradition of ceremonies celebrating everything from harvests to initiations. If your visit aligns with one, consider yourself fortunate to witness authentic local culture.

Practical Tips for Visiting Casamance

1. **Travel Safety**: While the region is largely peaceful, check for updates on local conditions, especially near the Guinea-Bissau border.
2. **Pack Light and Practical**: Bring mosquito repellent, lightweight clothing, and comfortable walking shoes.
3. **Respect Local Customs**: Always ask for permission before photographing people or sacred sites.

Pink Lake (Lac Retba)

Pink Lake (Lac Retba), is a marvel of nature known for its stunning pink hues and high salt content. Located just 35 kilometers northeast of Dakar, this UNESCO-nominated site offers a unique combination of natural beauty, cultural experiences, and adventure activities. Below is an in-depth guide covering everything you need to know for an unforgettable visit.

Key Information

- **Address**: Lac Retba, Rufisque Region, Senegal.
- **Opening Hours**: Open daily, 7:00 AM – 6:00 PM.
- **Entrance Fee**: Free access to the lake. Guided tours or activities are typically XOF 5,000 – XOF 15,000 per person.
- **Best Time to Visit**: November to May (dry season), when the lake's pink color is at its most vibrant due to high salinity and sunlight.

What Makes Pink Lake Unique?

The Phenomenon of the Pink Hue

The lake's distinctive pink coloration is caused by the presence of *Dunaliella salina*, a type of algae that thrives in its saline waters. These algae produce beta-carotene, a pigment that gives the lake its striking hue. The intensity of the color varies depending on sunlight, wind, and water levels, appearing most vivid under bright sunlight.

High Salt Content

Pink Lake has a salinity level of up to 40%, rivaling that of the Dead Sea. The high salt concentration allows visitors to float effortlessly on the water, a truly unique experience.

Things to Do at Pink Lake

1. Guided Tours of the Lake

- Local guides offer insightful tours explaining the lake's unique ecology and the traditional salt-harvesting process.
  - **Pricing**: XOF 10,000 – XOF 15,000 per group.
  - **Duration**: 1-2 hours.

2. Floating in the Saline Waters

- Floating in Pink Lake is an experience you shouldn't miss.
  - **What to Expect**: The high salinity ensures you float effortlessly, but avoid submerging your head as the water can irritate your eyes and skin.
  - **Tip**: Bring a towel and freshwater to rinse off after your float.

3. Salt Harvesting Demonstrations

- Observe or participate in traditional salt collection, where locals use wooden boats and buckets to extract salt from the lakebed.
  - **Fee**: A small tip (XOF 2,000 – XOF 5,000) to the harvesters is appreciated for demonstrations.

4. Quad Biking and Camel Rides

- **Quad Biking**: Explore the lake's perimeter and nearby sand dunes.
  - **Rental Fee**: XOF 15,000 – XOF 20,000 for a 30-minute ride.
- **Camel Rides**: Enjoy a leisurely ride along the shoreline.
  - **Cost**: XOF 5,000 per person.

5. Visit Nearby Villages

- Explore local villages to experience Senegalese culture, traditional crafts, and hospitality. Arrange for village tours through your guide or hotel.

Dining Options Near Pink Lake

1. **Chez Salim Restaurant**

   o **Location**: Near the lake's western shore.

   o **Specialties**: Fresh seafood, grilled fish, and Senegalese specialties like *thiéboudienne* (rice and fish).

   o **Pricing**: XOF 3,000 – XOF 8,000 per dish.

   o **Opening Hours**: Daily, 10:00 AM – 10:00 PM.

2. **Le Tranquille**

   o **Location**: Along the lakeside road.

   o **Ambiance**: Outdoor seating with views of the lake.

   o **Menu**: Local and international dishes.

   o **Pricing**: XOF 4,000 – XOF 9,000 per meal.

3. **Lodge du Lac**

   o **Cuisine**: French-inspired meals and cocktails.

   o **Perfect For**: Romantic dinners with a view of the sunset over the lake.

   o **Pricing**: XOF 6,000 – XOF 15,000.

Accommodation Options Near Pink Lake

1. **Hotel Le Trarza**

   o **Address**: Route de Lac Rose, Rufisque.

   o **Room Rates**: XOF 25,000 – XOF 50,000 per night.

- Facilities: Pool, lake-view rooms, and a restaurant.
2. **Chez Salim Lodge**
   - **Address**: Village Niaga, near Lac Retba.
   - **Room Rates**: XOF 30,000 – XOF 70,000 per night.
   - **Highlights**: Rustic charm, proximity to the lake, and guided tour packages.
3. **Les Cristaux Roses**
   - **Address**: Village Niaga.
   - **Room Rates**: XOF 20,000 – XOF 40,000 per night.
   - **Features**: Affordable guesthouse with basic amenities and friendly staff.

Travel Tips for Visiting Pink Lake

1. **Plan for Sun Protection**:
   - Bring sunscreen, a hat, and sunglasses to protect against the intense sun.
2. **Bring Cash**:
   - Many vendors and small establishments near the lake do not accept credit cards. Carry smaller denominations for tips and small purchases.
3. **Rinse Off After Floating**:
   - The salty water can be harsh on your skin, so rinse thoroughly after floating in the lake.
4. **Visit During Morning or Late Afternoon**:
   - These times offer the best lighting for photos and cooler temperatures for exploring.
5. **Respect Local Customs**:

- Dress modestly, especially if visiting nearby villages, and always ask for permission before taking photos of locals.

How to Get to Pink Lake

From Dakar:

- **Distance**: 35 kilometers northeast.
- **By Car**:
    - Duration: Approximately 1 hour.
    - Route: Take the N1 highway towards Rufisque and follow signs for Lac Retba.
- **By Taxi**:
    - Cost: XOF 10,000 – XOF 15,000 for a one-way trip.
- **By Public Transport**:
    - Take a shared taxi or minibus from Dakar to Rufisque (XOF 1,000), then hire a taxi to the lake (XOF 3,000).

Organized Tours:

- Many Dakar-based tour operators offer day trips to Pink Lake, often combined with visits to nearby beaches or cultural sites.
    - **Cost**: XOF 20,000 – XOF 50,000 per person, depending on the itinerary.

Nearby Attractions to Explore

1. **Atlantic Ocean Beaches**
    - Plage de Yoff and Plage de Ngor are excellent for relaxing after a day at the lake.
2. **Bandia Reserve**

- Located about 60 kilometers from Pink Lake, it offers a chance to see African wildlife such as giraffes, zebras, and rhinoceroses.
- **Entry Fee**: XOF 12,000 per person.

3. **Thiès Craft Market**
   - Known for its vibrant textiles, jewelry, and handmade goods.
   - **Distance**: 30 kilometers from Pink Lake.

4.6 Sine-Saloum Delta: Natural Beauty and Wildlife

The **Sine-Saloum Delta** is one of Senegal's most breathtaking natural treasures. Located where the Sine and Saloum Rivers meet before emptying into the Atlantic Ocean, this UNESCO World Heritage Site is a paradise of mangroves, lagoons, islands, and cultural heritage. It offers an unparalleled experience for nature lovers, history enthusiasts, and adventure seekers alike.

Getting There

- **Address**: Sine-Saloum Delta, Fatick Region, Senegal.
- **Coordinates**: Approximately 14.0991° N, 16.7522° W.
- **Nearest Major City**: Found about 150 km southeast of Dakar.

Transportation Options

1. **By Car**:
   - Route: Take the N1 highway from Dakar to Fatick, then continue southward on secondary roads to reach key towns like Ndangane or Toubakouta.
   - Road Condition: Paved roads until Fatick, then dirt roads in some parts. A 4x4 is recommended for remote areas.

2. **By Public Transport**:
   - o **Ndiaga Ndiaye minibuses** or **Sept-Places taxis** from Dakar to Fatick or Kaolack, followed by local transport to your destination.
   - o Cost: Around XOF 3,000 - XOF 5,000 depending on the route.
3. **By Boat**:
   - o Many local operators offer boat transfers to specific islands within the delta from ports like Ndangane or Missirah.

Opening Times and Entry Fees

- **Opening Times**: Accessible year-round. Best visiting hours are between 6:00 AM and 6:00 PM.
- **Entry Fee**: No centralized entrance fee for the delta, but certain reserves or activities (e.g., guided tours) may cost:
  - o Guided Boat Tours: XOF 5,000 - XOF 15,000 per person.
  - o Village Access Fees (optional contributions): XOF 500 - XOF 1,000 per visitor.

What to See and Do in the Sine-Saloum Delta

1. Explore the Natural Beauty

- **Mangrove Forests**:
  - o The delta is dominated by dense mangroves, home to a variety of wildlife. Explore these labyrinthine waterways by canoe or pirogue (traditional wooden boat).
- **Birdwatching**:

- Sine-Saloum is a birdwatcher's paradise, with over **400 bird species**. Highlights include pelicans, flamingos, herons, and African fish eagles.
    - Best Spots: Mar Lodj Island, Saloum National Park.
- **Fishing Villages**:
    - Visit traditional Serer and Mandinka fishing villages to see the daily life of local communities and their sustainable fishing practices.

2. Visit Historical and Cultural Sites

- **Shell Middens (Ancient Burial Mounds)**:
    - These archaeological sites contain layers of shells and artifacts, revealing the delta's rich history.
    - Key Locations: Joal-Fadiouth (Shell Island), Missirah.
- **Traditional Villages**:
    - Villages like Mar Lodj offer insight into Serer spirituality and culture, with sacred baobab trees and churches blending local traditions with Christianity.

3. Water-Based Activities

- **Boat Tours**:
    - Hop on a motorized or paddle-powered pirogue to explore the waterways, spot dolphins, and visit hidden islands.
    - Cost: XOF 5,000 - XOF 15,000 per person for a half-day tour.
- **Kayaking and Canoeing**:
    - Ideal for solo travelers and small groups seeking a tranquil exploration of lagoons and mangroves.
- **Fishing**:

- Try your hand at sport fishing or traditional net fishing. Fishing trips can be arranged through local operators in Ndangane or Toubakouta.

4. Wildlife and Ecotourism

- **Saloum Delta National Park**:
    - A designated biosphere reserve, this park is teeming with wildlife, including monkeys, manatees, and crocodiles.

- **Island Hopping**:
    - Discover islands like Sippo, Dassilame, and Gandoul, each with unique ecosystems and cultural significance.

Dining Options

Savor the flavors of the delta's fresh seafood and traditional Senegalese cuisine.

1. Popular Restaurants

- **Chez Aicha (Ndangane)**
    - **Specialties**: Grilled fish, shrimp, and yassa poulet (chicken in onion-lemon sauce).
    - **Pricing**: XOF 3,000 - XOF 7,000 per dish.
    - **Opening Hours**: Daily, 11:00 AM - 10:00 PM.

- **Keur Saloum (Toubakouta)**
    - **Specialties**: Local fish soup, bouye (baobab juice).
    - **Pricing**: XOF 4,000 - XOF 10,000.
    - **Opening Hours**: Daily, 12:00 PM - 9:00 PM.

2. Must-Try Dishes

- **Thieboudienne**: Senegal's iconic rice and fish dish.

- **Café Touba**: A spiced coffee drink, often served at roadside stalls.

Accommodation Options

Stay close to the delta's beauty with these curated lodging options.

1. Lodges and Hotels

- **Les Collines de Niassam**
    - **Location**: Palmarin.
    - **Features**: Eco-friendly bungalows and treehouses with stunning lagoon views.
    - **Pricing**: XOF 50,000 - XOF 100,000 per night.
- **Ecolodge de Simal**
    - **Location**: Simal, near Ndangane.
    - **Features**: Riverside chalets, on-site canoe rentals, and local cuisine.
    - **Pricing**: XOF 40,000 - XOF 80,000 per night.

2. Budget-Friendly Options

- **Campements Villageois**
    - Community-run guesthouses offering simple but comfortable accommodations.
    - Cost: XOF 10,000 - XOF 25,000 per night.

Best Time to Visit

- **Dry Season (November to May)**: Ideal for birdwatching, boat tours, and road travel due to dry conditions.
- **Rainy Season (June to October)**: Lush landscapes and fewer tourists, but some roads and trails may be inaccessible.

Practical Tips for Visiting the Sine-Saloum Delta

1. **Pack Smart**: Lightweight, breathable clothing, insect repellent, and waterproof footwear are essential.

2. **Respect Local Customs**: Always ask for permission before taking photos of people or sacred sites.

3. **Hire a Guide**: Local guides can enrich your experience by sharing in-depth knowledge of the delta's ecology and culture.

CHAPTER 5.

CULTURAL EXPERIENCES

Senegalese Music and Dance

Key Venues for Senegalese Music and Dance

1. Village des Arts, Dakar

- **Address**: Route de l'Aéroport, Dakar.
- **Opening Times**: Monday to Saturday, 10:00 AM - 6:00 PM.
- **Pricing**: Free entry, workshops from XOF 5,000.
- **What to Expect**: Live performances, drum circles, and dance workshops hosted by local artists.

2. Just 4 U, Dakar

- **Address**: Avenue Cheikh Anta Diop, Dakar.
- **Opening Times**: 8:00 PM till late (live music nights every Friday and Saturday).
- **Pricing**: Entry XOF 2,000 - XOF 5,000.
- **What to Expect**: Senegal's best mbalax artists perform here regularly, creating a dynamic and intimate setting for music enthusiasts.

3. Théâtre Sorano, Dakar

- **Address**: Rue de la République, Dakar.
- **Opening Times**: Events scheduled weekly, primarily evenings.

- **Pricing**: Tickets range from XOF 3,000 to XOF 10,000.
- **What to Expect**: Traditional and contemporary dance performances by professional troupes.

4. Alliance Franco-Sénégalaise, Saint-Louis
- **Address**: Rue Blanchot, Saint-Louis.
- **Opening Times**: Variable, depending on events.
- **Pricing**: Workshops start at XOF 4,000.
- **What to Expect**: An arts hub offering classes, concerts, and exhibitions featuring Senegalese culture.

Traditional Senegalese Music: A Deep Dive

1. Mbalax: The Heartbeat of Senegal
- **What It Is**: Mbalax (pronounced "mm-bal-ahkh") is Senegal's signature music genre, fusing traditional sabar drum rhythms with Afro-Cuban, jazz, and funk influences.
- **Key Artists**: Youssou N'Dour, Omar Pene, Viviane Chidid.

2. The Role of Griots
- **Who They Are**: Griots, or "jeli," are hereditary storytellers, musicians, and historians. They preserve oral traditions through songs and spoken word.
- **Experience It**: Visit the villages of Kaolack or Toubacouta for intimate griot performances.

3. Sabar Drumming
- **What It Is**: A percussive style using hand-carved sabar drums. This music often accompanies community events such as weddings and naming ceremonies.
- **Where to Learn**: Drum workshops are held at the **Village des Arts** in Dakar and in **Toubab Dialaw**.

Contemporary Senegalese Music

1. Hip Hop and Urban Beats

- Senegal is a hub for West African hip hop, addressing themes of social justice and youth empowerment.
- **Top Venues**:
    - **Thiossane Nightclub** in Dakar, owned by Youssou N'Dour.
    - **Le Must**, a popular spot for underground hip hop.

2. Afro-Jazz Fusion

- Bands like Orchestra Baobab bring a fusion of traditional Senegalese sounds with Cuban and jazz influences.
- **Catch Live Shows**: Look for performances at **Le Penc Mi** or **Institut Français de Dakar**.

Dance: The Soul of Senegalese Culture

1. Sabar Dance

- **What It Is**: Energetic and improvisational, sabar dance accompanies sabar drumming. Dancers showcase athleticism through jumps and spins.
- **Where to Learn**:
    - **Ecole des Sables**, Toubab Dialaw.
        - **Workshops**: From XOF 10,000 per session.
        - **Accommodation**: On-site eco-lodges start at XOF 30,000 per night.

2. Lambaan

- **What It Is**: A traditional dance performed during celebrations, characterized by flowing arm movements and intricate footwork.
- **Experience It**: Visit Saint-Louis during cultural festivals to witness Lambaan performances.

3. Tassu

- **What It Is**: A unique blend of spoken word and rhythm, often performed by women during ceremonies.
- **Where to See It**: Community gatherings in villages such as Joal-Fadiouth.

Festivals Showcasing Music and Dance

1. Saint-Louis Jazz Festival

- **Location**: Saint-Louis.
- **Timing**: Annually in May.
- **Pricing**: Passes range from XOF 15,000 to XOF 50,000.
- **What to Expect**: A week-long celebration of Afro-jazz and fusion genres with performances by international and local artists.

2. Dakar Music Festival

- **Location**: Various venues across Dakar.
- **Timing**: December.
- **What to Expect**: Mbalax, hip hop, and Afrobeat performances.

3. Festival de l'Eau

- **Location**: Sine-Saloum Delta.
- **Timing**: October.

- **What to Expect**: Traditional music and dance celebrating the delta's waterways.

Dining and Music: The Perfect Pairing

1. Alkimia, Dakar

- **Specialty**: Gourmet dishes with live acoustic music performances.
- **Address**: Rue de Pointe des Almadies, Dakar.
- **Pricing**: XOF 15,000 - XOF 40,000 per meal.
- **Opening Hours**: Daily, 6:00 PM - Midnight.

2. Le Djembé, Toubab Dialaw

- **Specialty**: Traditional Senegalese meals accompanied by live sabar drumming.
- **Pricing**: XOF 5,000 - XOF 15,000.
- **Opening Hours**: 12:00 PM - 10:00 PM.

Practical Tips for Enjoying Music and Dance

1. **Immerse Yourself**: Don't just watch; participate in dance workshops or drum circles for an authentic experience.
2. **Respect the Art**: Always ask permission before recording performances, especially in villages.
3. **Dress Comfortably**: Wear breathable clothes and bring a reusable water bottle, as events often last hours.

Art and Craft Markets

Key Art and Craft Markets in Senegal

1. Soumbedioune Artisan Market (Dakar)

- **Address**: Corniche Ouest, Soumbedioune, Dakar, Senegal.
- **Opening Hours**: Daily, 9:00 AM – 8:00 PM.
- **Pricing**: Entry is free; prices for items range from XOF 500 to XOF 200,000, depending on the craft.

Overview: Soumbedioune is one of Dakar's most famous artisan markets, located along the scenic Corniche road. It is renowned for its wide array of handmade goods, including leatherwork, wood carvings, and traditional jewelry.

What to Explore:

- **Textiles**: Browse stalls selling vibrant wax print fabrics and handwoven materials.
- **Wooden Sculptures**: From small trinkets to large, intricately carved statues representing Senegalese culture.
- **Custom Orders**: Many artisans allow you to place bespoke orders, such as custom-fitted leather sandals.

Dining Nearby:

- **La Corniche Restaurant**: Serves fresh seafood with views of the ocean. Average cost: XOF 5,000 - XOF 15,000 per meal.

Accommodation:

- **Hotel Jardin Savana Dakar**: A mid-range option just 10 minutes from the market. Prices start at XOF 50,000 per night.

---

2. Village des Arts (Dakar)

- **Address**: Rue des Ecrivains, Dakar, Senegal.

- **Opening Hours**: Tuesday – Sunday, 10:00 AM – 6:00 PM. Closed on Mondays.
- **Pricing**: Entry is free; workshops and artwork are priced individually, starting at XOF 10,000.

Overview: More than just a market, Village des Arts is a hub for creativity. Home to over 50 resident artists, it offers a mix of galleries, studios, and outdoor displays.

What to Explore:

- **Live Art Creation**: Watch painters, sculptors, and potters work in their studios.
- **Art Exhibitions**: Regularly rotating displays of contemporary Senegalese art.
- **Workshops**: Participate in hands-on art classes led by local experts.

Dining Nearby:

- **Le Patio**: A cozy café offering light snacks and drinks. Average cost: XOF 3,000 - XOF 7,000.

Accommodation:

- **Radisson Blu Hotel Dakar Sea Plaza**: A luxury hotel just 15 minutes away. Prices start at XOF 150,000 per night.

---

3. Marché HLM (Dakar)

- **Address**: Avenue Lamine Guèye, Dakar, Senegal.
- **Opening Hours**: Monday – Saturday, 8:00 AM – 7:00 PM. Closed on Sundays.
- **Pricing**: No entry fee; fabric prices range from XOF 2,000 per meter for simple patterns to XOF 20,000 for premium materials.

Overview: Known for its extraordinary collection of fabrics, Marché HLM is a go-to destination for anyone interested in Senegal's vibrant textile tradition.

What to Explore:

- **Wax Prints**: Bold, colorful designs that are central to West African fashion.
- **Custom Tailoring**: Many vendors offer on-the-spot tailoring services for traditional outfits.
- **Accessories**: Handbags, headwraps, and other items crafted from local fabrics.

Dining Nearby:

- **Chez Fatou**: A family-run eatery serving traditional Senegalese dishes. Average cost: XOF 2,000 - XOF 5,000 per meal.

Accommodation:

- **Résidence Mamoune**: A comfortable budget option near the market. Prices start at XOF 25,000 per night.

---

4. Saint-Louis Artisans' Market

- **Address**: Rue Blaise Diagne, Saint-Louis, Senegal.
- **Opening Hours**: Daily, 9:00 AM – 7:00 PM.
- **Pricing**: Entry is free; artwork and crafts are priced from XOF 1,000 to XOF 50,000.

Overview: Located in Senegal's historic city of Saint-Louis, this market reflects the region's rich cultural heritage.

What to Explore:

- **Metalwork**: Stunning sculptures and ornaments crafted from recycled materials.
- **Paintings**: Vibrant depictions of Senegalese life by local artists.

- **Traditional Musical Instruments**: Handcrafted drums and koras (African harps).

Dining Nearby:
- **Restaurant Flamingo**: Offers riverfront dining with traditional and international cuisine. Average cost: XOF 4,000 - XOF 10,000.

Accommodation:
- **Hotel de La Poste**: A historic hotel in the heart of Saint-Louis. Prices start at XOF 45,000 per night.

---

5. Casamance Craft Markets

- **Key Locations**: Ziguinchor, Cap Skirring, Oussouye.
- **Opening Hours**: Daily, 8:00 AM – 6:00 PM.
- **Pricing**: Crafts typically range from XOF 1,000 to XOF 30,000.

Overview: The Casamance region is renowned for its unique artistic styles influenced by Diola culture.

What to Explore:
- **Basketry**: Beautifully woven baskets and mats made from natural fibers.
- **Beaded Jewelry**: Traditional designs incorporating shells and seeds.
- **Masks and Ritual Objects**: Intricately carved items used in Diola ceremonies.

Dining Nearby:
- **Les Palétuviers**: Offers delicious seafood and stunning views of the mangroves. Average cost: XOF 6,000 - XOF 12,000 per meal.

Accommodation:

- **Cap Skirring Resort**: A luxury beachfront resort. Prices start at XOF 100,000 per night.

Tips for Shopping at Art and Craft Markets

1. **Bargaining**:
   - Negotiation is expected and part of the shopping experience. Start by offering half of the asking price and work your way up.

2. **Quality Check**:
   - Inspect items for authenticity, especially textiles and jewelry. Genuine wax prints have vibrant colors on both sides of the fabric.

3. **Support Local Artisans**:
   - Opt for stalls run by the artisans themselves rather than middlemen.

4. **Bring Cash**:
   - Most markets operate on a cash-only basis. Small denominations are handy for easier transactions.

Traditional Ceremonies and Festivals

1. Traditional Ceremonies

Naming Ceremonies (Ngente)

Address: Throughout Senegal, especially in Serer and Wolof communities. Often held in family homes or village centers.

Timing: Held seven days after a child's birth.

Entry Fee: Free; attendees are often family, friends, or community members, but visitors are welcome with an invitation or guide.

Description:

The **Ngente** is a cherished Senegalese tradition where a newborn is officially given a name. The ceremony is steeped in spirituality, with blessings from elders, prayers, and the recitation of Quranic verses.

Highlights:

- **Sheep Sacrifice**: A sheep is often sacrificed as a symbol of gratitude and protection for the child.
- **Traditional Music and Dance**: Griot performers use drums and kora (a string instrument) to provide a lively soundtrack.
- **Food Sharing**: Visitors are served communal dishes like thieboudienne (rice and fish) and sweets like thiakry (sweet millet pudding).

Initiation Rites

Location: Rural areas, especially in Casamance and among Serer and Mandinka communities.

Timing: Seasonal; varies depending on ethnic group traditions.

Entry Fee: Typically not open to tourists but can be observed through cultural tours.

Description:

Initiation rites mark the transition from childhood to adulthood. These ceremonies are deeply symbolic and involve storytelling, communal bonding, and instruction in community values.

Key Features:

- **Sacred Forests**: Many rituals occur in designated sacred groves, emphasizing harmony with nature.
- **Cultural Storytelling**: Elders pass down oral histories and life lessons.

2. Festivals in Senegal

Saint-Louis Jazz Festival

Address: Saint-Louis Island, Saint-Louis.

Timing: Annually in May (exact dates vary).

Entry Fee:

- General Admission: XOF 5,000 - XOF 10,000 per day.
- VIP Pass: XOF 20,000 - XOF 50,000.

Description:

One of Africa's most prestigious music festivals, the Saint-Louis Jazz Festival celebrates jazz and its fusion with African rhythms.

What to Expect:

- **Performances**: Renowned local and international artists perform at venues across Saint-Louis, from open-air stages to intimate clubs.
- **Workshops and Exhibits**: Music workshops, art exhibitions, and cultural forums run alongside the concerts.
- **Dining**: Savor regional cuisine at nearby eateries like **Flamingo** (XOF 6,000 - XOF 15,000).

Dakar Biennale (Dak'Art)

Address: Various locations in Dakar, including the Museum of Black Civilizations and IFAN Museum.

Timing: Biennially, from May to June.

Entry Fee:

- General Admission: XOF 1,000 - XOF 3,000 per venue.
- Free entry for outdoor exhibits.

Description:

The **Dakar Biennale** is West Africa's premier art festival, showcasing contemporary African art across diverse mediums.

Key Highlights:

- **Art Exhibitions**: Paintings, sculptures, and installations by emerging and established artists.
- **Performance Art**: Live performances and workshops emphasizing African themes.

Tabaski (Eid al-Adha)

Location: Nationwide; celebrated in homes, mosques, and public spaces.

Timing: Based on the Islamic lunar calendar.

Entry Fee: Free; participate as a guest or with a local guide.

Description:

Tabaski, or Eid al-Adha, is a deeply spiritual Islamic festival commemorating Abraham's willingness to sacrifice his son. Families come together for prayers, feasts, and acts of charity.

What to Witness:

- **Morning Prayers**: Thousands gather in mosques for communal prayers.
- **Sheep Sacrifice**: Each household sacrifices a sheep, symbolizing devotion and obedience to God.
- **Feasting**: Families share traditional dishes like maafe (peanut stew) and grilled meat.

Festival of the Desert (Festival du Sahel)

Address: Lompoul Desert, Louga Region.

Timing: Annually in December.

Entry Fee:

- General Admission: XOF 10,000 - XOF 30,000.

- Includes access to performances and activities.

Description:

This unique festival blends music, poetry, and storytelling in the mesmerizing Lompoul Desert.

Activities:

- **Traditional Music**: Performances by Fulani and Wolof musicians.
- **Camel Rides**: Explore the dunes on camelback.
- **Overnight Stay**: Stay in luxury tents (XOF 50,000 - XOF 100,000 per night).

---

3. Cultural Etiquette for Festivals and Ceremonies

1. **Dress Appropriately**: Modest clothing is essential, especially for religious events. Women may need to cover their heads during Islamic ceremonies.
2. **Respect Rituals**: Observe silently during prayers or solemn moments, and refrain from taking photos unless permitted.
3. **Engage with Locals**: Interact with locals to gain deeper insights into the traditions and their significance.

---

4. Dining Options During Festivals

Festivals and ceremonies are often accompanied by feasts showcasing Senegalese culinary delights.

1. Street Food

- **Grilled Fish**: Freshly caught and cooked over open flames.
- **Fataya**: Fried pastries filled with meat or fish.
- **Bissap**: A refreshing hibiscus drink, often sold by street vendors.

123

2. Restaurants Near Festival Locations

- **Le Diamarek (Saint-Louis)**
  - ○ **Specialties**: Seafood platters, Senegalese desserts.
  - ○ **Pricing**: XOF 7,000 - XOF 15,000 per meal.
- **Noflaye Beach (Dakar)**
  - ○ **Specialties**: Grilled seafood, maafe.
  - ○ **Pricing**: XOF 6,000 - XOF 12,000 per dish.

---

5. Accommodation During Festivals

1. Hotels Near Event Venues

- **Hotel de la Poste (Saint-Louis)**
  - ○ **Pricing**: XOF 45,000 - XOF 80,000 per night.
- **Radisson Blu Hotel (Dakar)**
  - ○ **Pricing**: XOF 90,000 - XOF 150,000 per night.

2. Budget Lodging

- **Campements Villageois**: Affordable and located near rural festival venues.
  - ○ **Pricing**: XOF 10,000 - XOF 20,000 per night.

Best Time to Experience Senegalese Ceremonies and Festivals

- Dry Season (November to May): Ideal for traveling to rural festivals like the Festival of the Desert.
- Islamic Calendar Holidays: Dates vary; check in advance for events like Tabaski.

CHAPTER 6.

EXPLORING SENEGAL'S NATURAL BEAUTY

Niokolo-Koba National Park

Niokolo-Koba National Park is one of Senegal's premier destinations for wildlife enthusiasts and nature lovers. Located in the southeastern part of the country, this UNESCO World Heritage Site is a sprawling expanse of diverse ecosystems, offering visitors a chance to experience Senegal's rich biodiversity in its raw, untouched form.

- **Address**: Niokolo-Koba National Park, Tambacounda Region, Senegal.
- **Coordinates**: Approximately 13.0604° N, 13.3085° W.
- **Nearest City**: Tambacounda (about 40 km away).
- **Opening Hours**: Daily from 6:00 AM to 6:00 PM.
- **Entrance Fees**:
    - Adults: XOF 5,000.
    - Children (under 12): XOF 2,500.
    - Vehicle Entry: XOF 3,000.
    - Guide Fee: XOF 10,000 - XOF 15,000 per day.

Contact Information

- **Park Office**:
    - **Location**: Main entrance near Dar Salam village.
    - **Phone**: +221 33 981 2020.

How to Get There

By Car

- From **Dakar**: The drive to Tambacounda takes approximately 9-10 hours via the N1 highway. From Tambacounda, continue south on a well-marked road to reach the park entrance near Dar Salam.
- **Road Conditions**: Paved roads until Tambacounda; gravel and dirt roads within the park. A 4x4 vehicle is recommended for deeper exploration.

By Public Transport

- **Buses** and **Sept-Places Taxis**: Available from Dakar to Tambacounda. From Tambacounda, hire a local taxi to reach the park entrance.
- **Cost**: XOF 8,000 - XOF 15,000 for the journey to Tambacounda.

What to See and Do in Niokolo-Koba National Park

1. Wildlife Safaris

Niokolo-Koba is home to over 80 species of mammals, 330 bird species, and countless reptiles, amphibians, and fish.

- **Key Animals**:
    - **Large Mammals**: Lions, leopards, elephants (rare sightings), hippos, and buffalo.

- o **Antelopes**: Derby elands (the world's largest antelope), waterbucks, and bushbucks.
  - o **Primates**: Baboons, patas monkeys, and green vervet monkeys.
  - o **Reptiles**: Nile crocodiles and various snake species.
- **Best Safari Routes**:
  - o The **Simenti Zone**: Known for its concentration of wildlife and stunning river views.
  - o The **Bafoulabé Area**: A hotspot for birdwatching.

2. Birdwatching

Bird enthusiasts can expect a spectacular experience, with species like Abyssinian ground hornbills, guinea fowls, and saddle-billed storks commonly spotted.

- **Best Viewing Times**: Early morning and late afternoon.

3. Hiking and Trekking

Guided hikes through the park's diverse landscapes include savannahs, gallery forests, and wetlands.

- **Popular Trails**:
  - o **Mount Assirik**: A challenging trek offering panoramic views of the park.
  - o **Wetlands Walk**: Ideal for spotting hippos and crocodiles near water bodies.

4. River Excursions

Boat tours on the **Gambia River**, which flows through the park, provide a unique perspective of the flora and fauna.

- **Cost**: XOF 10,000 - XOF 20,000 per person for a half-day tour.

Best Time to Visit

- **Dry Season (November to May)**: Optimal for wildlife spotting as animals gather around waterholes.

- **Rainy Season (June to October)**: The park transforms into a lush green paradise, but some trails may be inaccessible due to flooding.

Dining Options Near the Park

1. Inside the Park

- **Simenti Camp Dining Area**
    - **Cuisine**: Traditional Senegalese dishes like thieboudienne (rice and fish) and yassa poulet (chicken with onions).
    - **Pricing**: XOF 2,500 - XOF 5,000 per meal.
    - **Opening Hours**: Daily, 7:00 AM - 9:00 PM.

2. Nearby Villages

- **Chez Fanta (Dar Salam)**
    - **Specialties**: Grilled fish, plantains, and fresh juices.
    - **Pricing**: XOF 2,000 - XOF 4,000.

Accommodation Options

1. Inside the Park

- **Simenti Hotel**
    - **Location**: Simenti Zone.
    - **Features**: Basic rooms with river views, guided safari packages.
    - **Pricing**: From XOF 25,000 per night.

2. Outside the Park

- **Campement Wassadou**
    - o **Location**: 10 km from the park entrance.
    - o **Features**: Riverside bungalows, birdwatching decks.
    - o **Pricing**: XOF 20,000 - XOF 50,000 per night.

Practical Tips for Visiting

1. **Hire a Guide**: Guides are mandatory for safaris and treks to ensure safety and maximize wildlife sightings.
2. **What to Bring**:
    - o Binoculars for birdwatching.
    - o Sun protection (hat, sunscreen).
    - o Insect repellent to ward off mosquitoes.
    - o Comfortable clothing and sturdy hiking shoes.
3. **Park Rules**:
    - o Stay within designated areas to protect wildlife and ecosystems.
    - o Avoid loud noises that can disturb animals.

Unique Experiences

Cultural Encounters

- Visit nearby **Mandinka** and **Fulani villages** for a glimpse into traditional lifestyles.

Night Safari

- Experience the thrill of spotting nocturnal animals like bush babies and hyenas.

Photography Workshops

- Perfect for amateur and professional photographers to capture the park's diverse landscapes and wildlife.

Djoudj Bird Sanctuary

The **Djoudj Bird Sanctuary**, or Parc National des Oiseaux du Djoudj, is a world-renowned UNESCO World Heritage Site and a vital stopover for millions of migratory birds. Located in northern Senegal, near the border with Mauritania, it is an extraordinary ecosystem that offers one of the most spectacular birdwatching experiences in Africa. Spanning over 16,000 hectares, this wetland area is a haven for both wildlife and those who appreciate the serene beauty of untouched nature.

Key Information

- **Address**: Djoudj Bird Sanctuary, Saint-Louis Region, Senegal.
- **Opening Times**: Open daily from **8:00 AM to 6:00 PM** (Seasonal adjustments may apply).
- **Best Visiting Months**: **November to March** for peak bird activity.
- **Entry Fees**:
  - **Adults**: XOF 2,000 per person.
  - **Children**: XOF 1,000 per person.
  - Additional fees may apply for boat tours.
- **How to Get There**:
  - **From Saint-Louis**: Approximately 60 km southeast (about 1.5 hours by car).
  - **Transport Options**:

- Private cars or taxis are recommended.
- Guided tours often include transportation from Saint-Louis.

What Makes Djoudj Bird Sanctuary Unique?

Djoudj is more than a birdwatcher's paradise—it is a critical breeding and wintering ground for over **1.5 million birds** across **400 species**. Its location on the edge of the Sahara Desert makes it a vital freshwater resource in the region.

1. Ecological Importance

- **Wetlands**: Comprising a network of lakes, ponds, and streams, Djoudj provides essential habitats for both migratory and resident species.
- **Conservation**: The sanctuary is part of a larger effort to protect biodiversity in the Sahel region, ensuring the survival of rare and endangered species.

2. Seasonal Highlights

- **November to March**: Witness flocks of flamingos, pelicans, herons, and cormorants in their full glory.
- **June to September**: The rainy season transforms the park into a lush, green haven, attracting species like African fish eagles and jacanas.

Must-See Attractions and Experiences

1. Birdwatching

Djoudj is best known for its massive colonies of **great white pelicans** and **lesser flamingos**.

- **Top Viewing Points:**

- Observation towers around the central lake provide panoramic views.
- Boat tours offer up-close encounters with pelicans, ducks, and other waterfowl.
- **Key Species to Spot**:
  - **Migratory Birds**: Garganey, Northern pintail, and Eurasian wigeon.
  - **Resident Birds**: African darter, purple heron, and black-crowned crane.

2. Boat Tours

- A guided boat ride through the sanctuary's waterways is the best way to explore its diverse habitats.
- **Cost**: XOF 5,000–10,000 per person for a 1–2 hour tour.
- **What to Expect**: Glide through calm waters, observe nesting sites, and photograph birds in their natural environment.

3. Wildlife Beyond Birds

Djoudj is not just about avian wonders. Keep an eye out for:

- **Mammals**: Warthogs, African golden wolves, and river otters.
- **Reptiles**: Nile crocodiles and monitor lizards.

4. Photography and Nature Walks

- Bring a telephoto lens for stunning shots of birds in flight and vibrant sunsets over the wetlands.
- Guided nature walks are available, providing insights into the park's ecology and conservation efforts.

Dining Options Near Djoudj

While the sanctuary itself does not have extensive dining facilities, nearby towns like Saint-Louis offer great options for refueling after a day of exploration.

1. On-Site Amenities

- Small snack stalls near the entrance sell beverages, sandwiches, and local snacks.
- It's recommended to carry your own picnic if spending the entire day at the sanctuary.

2. Restaurants in Saint-Louis

- **Flamingo Restaurant**
    - **Address**: Quai Henri Jay, Saint-Louis.
    - **Specialties**: Grilled fish, Senegalese rice dishes, and fresh juices.
    - **Pricing**: XOF 5,000–10,000 per meal.
    - **Opening Hours**: Daily, 11:00 AM – 10:00 PM.
- **La Crepe Saint-Louisienne**
    - **Specialties**: Savory and sweet crepes, along with light refreshments.
    - **Pricing**: XOF 3,000–6,000.

Accommodation Near Djoudj Bird Sanctuary

Choose from comfortable lodges and eco-friendly stays within proximity to the sanctuary.

1. Djoudj Lodge

- **Location**: Near the park entrance.

- **Features**: Rustic bungalows with solar-powered amenities and guided tour packages.
- **Pricing**: XOF 25,000–50,000 per night.

2. Hotel de la Poste (Saint-Louis)

- **Address**: Quai Roume, Saint-Louis.
- **Features**: Colonial-era charm with modern comforts, ideal for exploring the region.
- **Pricing**: XOF 45,000–85,000 per night.

Best Time to Visit

- **Peak Season**: November to March for bird migrations.
- **Avoid**: May to October, when heavy rains can make some trails and roads inaccessible.

Practical Tips for Visiting Djoudj

1. **Prepare for the Elements**:
   - Wear lightweight clothing, a wide-brimmed hat, and sturdy walking shoes.
   - Bring sunscreen, insect repellent, and a refillable water bottle.

2. **Respect Wildlife**:
   - Maintain a safe distance from animals and avoid feeding them.
   - Use binoculars and cameras with zoom lenses to observe birds without disturbing them.

3. **Hire a Guide**:

o   Local guides are knowledgeable about the sanctuary's
        flora, fauna, and history, enhancing your visit.

Beyond Djoudj: Exploring the Saint-Louis Region

If time allows, consider extending your trip to explore other attractions near Djoudj Bird Sanctuary:

- **Langue de Barbarie National Park**: Located near Saint-Louis, this park offers pristine beaches and more birdwatching opportunities.

- **Saint-Louis Island**: A UNESCO World Heritage Site, known for its colonial architecture and vibrant cultural scene.

Petite Côte: Beach Escapes

The **Petite Côte**, or "Little Coast," stretches along Senegal's Atlantic shoreline, approximately 70 km south of Dakar. This breathtaking region is known for its golden beaches, vibrant fishing villages, luxurious resorts, and stunning natural reserves. A favorite among tourists and locals alike, the Petite Côte offers a blend of relaxation, adventure, and cultural discovery.

Key Information

- **Location**: South of Dakar, Senegal, from Rufisque to Joal-Fadiouth.

- **Opening Times**: Accessible year-round, with peak times being November to May during the dry season.

- **Pricing**: Entry to beaches and most villages is free. Guided tours, water sports, and reserves have fees ranging from XOF 5,000 to XOF 30,000.

Transportation

- **By Road**:
    - Route N1 connects Dakar to key destinations along the Petite Côte.
    - Travel Time: 1-2 hours by car from Dakar.
    - Cost: Private taxi from Dakar starts at XOF 20,000; shared buses cost XOF 2,000 - XOF 5,000.
- **By Air**:
    - Closest airport: Blaise Diagne International Airport in Diass (45 minutes from Saly).

Top Destinations Along the Petite Côte

1. Saly-Portudal: Senegal's Resort Capital

- **Address**: Saly-Portudal, Mbour Department, Senegal.
- **Opening Hours**: Hotels and beaches are open daily.
- **Pricing**: Beach access is free, while resorts offer day passes starting at XOF 10,000.

Highlights:

- **Luxury Resorts**: Stay at beachfront properties like **Royal Saly** or **Hotel Neptune** for premium amenities.
    - **Pricing**: XOF 50,000 - XOF 150,000 per night.
- **Water Sports**: Jet skiing, windsurfing, and catamaran rentals are popular.
    - **Pricing**: Activities start at XOF 10,000 per hour.
- **Nightlife**: Dance to mbalax music in clubs or enjoy a quiet evening at seaside lounges.

---

2. Mbour: Authentic Senegalese Fishing Town

- **Address**: Mbour, located 15 km south of Saly.
- **Opening Hours**: Fishing port operates daily from sunrise to sunset.
- **Pricing**: Guided tours of the fishing port start at XOF 3,000 per person.

Highlights:

- **Fishing Port**: Witness colorful pirogues returning with fresh catches and experience the bustling fish market.
- **Cultural Interaction**: Engage with fishermen and learn about traditional fishing methods.
- **Dining**: Visit **Chez Fatou** for freshly grilled fish (meals cost XOF 4,000 - XOF 8,000).

---

3. Joal-Fadiouth: The Shell Island

- **Address**: Joal-Fadiouth, located at the southern end of the Petite Côte.
- **Opening Hours**: Daily, 8:00 AM – 6:00 PM.
- **Pricing**: Entry fee for guided tours: XOF 5,000 per person.

Highlights:

- **Shell Island**: Entirely made of shells, this unique island hosts a peaceful cemetery where Muslims and Christians rest side by side.
- **Wooden Bridge**: A picturesque 500-meter bridge connects Joal to Fadiouth.
- **Boat Rides**: Take a traditional pirogue tour around the island for XOF 2,500 per person.

---

4. Bandia Wildlife Reserve

- **Address**: Located near the village of Bandia, 15 km from Saly.
- **Opening Hours**: Daily, 9:00 AM – 5:00 PM.
- **Pricing**:
  - Adults: XOF 12,000
  - Children: XOF 6,000
  - Vehicle rental with guide: XOF 40,000

Highlights:

- **Wildlife Safaris**: Spot giraffes, zebras, antelopes, monkeys, and rhinoceroses in their natural habitat.
- **Baobab Trees**: Explore ancient baobabs, some used as burial sites centuries ago.
- **Dining**: Enjoy meals at the **Bandia Reserve Restaurant**, overlooking a waterhole frequented by animals.

---

5. Popenguine Nature Reserve

- **Address**: Popenguine, approximately 70 km from Dakar.
- **Opening Hours**: Daily, 8:00 AM – 6:00 PM.
- **Pricing**: Guided tours start at XOF 7,500 per person.

Highlights:

- **Scenic Hiking Trails**: Traverse cliffs and rocky landscapes for panoramic ocean views.
- **Birdwatching**: Spot rare species like the white-breasted cormorant and pelicans.
- **Eco-Lodges**: Stay at community-managed lodges like **Keur Bernard** (XOF 15,000 - XOF 30,000 per night).

Activities Along the Petite Côte

1. Beach Relaxation

Golden sands and calm waters make beaches like **Plage de Saly** and **Plage de Somone** perfect for sunbathing and swimming.

2. Traditional Markets

- Visit the **Mbour Weekly Market** to shop for handicrafts, textiles, and spices.
- **Pricing**: Bargain for better deals; typical souvenirs cost XOF 1,000 - XOF 10,000.

3. Culinary Experiences

- Try Senegalese specialties like **thieboudienne** (rice and fish) and **yassa poulet** (chicken with lemon-onion sauce).
- Recommended Restaurants:
  - **La Riviera** (Saly): XOF 5,000 - XOF 12,000 per meal.
  - **Chez Ngor** (Somone): XOF 4,000 - XOF 10,000 per meal.

4. Art and Craft Workshops

- Learn batik-making or wood carving in workshops offered by local artists in Popenguine and Joal.

Best Time to Visit

- **Dry Season (November to May)**: Ideal for beach days, safaris, and hiking.
- **Rainy Season (June to October)**: Lush greenery and fewer tourists, though some roads may be muddy.

Accommodation Options

Luxury Resorts

- **Lamantin Beach Resort (Saly)**: Features private beaches, a spa, and gourmet dining.
    - **Pricing**: From XOF 80,000 per night.

Eco-Lodges

- **Les Manguiers de Guéréo (Somone)**: Nestled in a mangrove, offering sustainable stays.
    - **Pricing**: From XOF 40,000 per night.

Budget Stays

- **Chez Jules (Joal-Fadiouth)**: Affordable rooms with authentic local hospitality.
    - **Pricing**: From XOF 10,000 per night.

Tips for Travelers

1. **Pack Essentials**: Sunscreen, hats, and lightweight clothing for beach and safari days.
2. **Engage Locals**: Learn a few Wolof phrases like "Jërëjëf" (thank you) to show respect.
3. **Plan Ahead**: Book accommodations and guided tours during the peak season.

Fathala Wildlife Reserve

Fathala Wildlife Reserve is a sanctuary of biodiversity and an essential destination for anyone eager to explore Senegal's unique natural beauty. This reserve offers an immersive experience with West Africa's native wildlife, blending adventure, conservation, and relaxation in one extraordinary location.

Key Information

- **Address**: Fathala Wildlife Reserve, Karang, Fatick Region, Senegal.
- **Coordinates**: 13.6882° N, 16.4435° W.
- **Nearest Major City**: 12 km from Kaolack, Senegal, and near the Gambian border at Karang.
- **Opening Times**: Daily, 7:00 AM to 6:00 PM.
- **Pricing**:
  - **Game Drive**: XOF 15,000 - XOF 30,000 per person (varies based on group size and duration).
  - **Lion Walk Experience**: XOF 40,000 per person.
  - **Children under 12**: Discounted rates available.
- **Contact**: +221 77 450 42 65 or info@fathala.com

Getting to Fathala Wildlife Reserve

By Car

- From **Dakar**: Take the N1 highway to Kaolack, then continue south toward Karang. The drive takes approximately **4–5 hours**.
- From **Banjul, Gambia**: Cross the border at Karang, which is less than 1 hour from the reserve.

By Public Transport

- **Bush taxis** or **Ndiaga Ndiaye minibuses** connect Kaolack with Karang. From Karang, hire a private taxi for the short trip to Fathala.

What Makes Fathala Wildlife Reserve Special

Fathala is a **2,000-hectare reserve** that combines the preservation of native Senegalese flora and fauna with the reintroduction of iconic African wildlife. Visitors can encounter species such as antelopes, giraffes, zebras, rhinos, and lions while enjoying eco-friendly tourism.

1. Unique Wildlife Encounters

Fathala is renowned for its rare opportunities to see iconic African species in Senegal.

- **Antelopes and Gazelles**: Including species like the critically endangered **derby eland** and the majestic **roan antelope**.
- **Lions**: The reserve offers a thrilling **Lion Walk Experience**, where visitors can walk alongside lions in a controlled environment under the supervision of trained guides.
- **Birdlife**: Over 150 bird species inhabit the reserve, making it a paradise for birdwatchers.

Activities at Fathala Wildlife Reserve

1. Guided Game Drives

- **Overview**: Explore the reserve in open-top 4x4 vehicles, led by knowledgeable guides who share insights into the wildlife and ecology of the area.
- **Duration**: 2–3 hours.
- **Highlights**: Spotting giraffes grazing among the acacia trees, herds of zebras, and elusive bushbucks.

2. Lion Walk Experience

- **Unique Adventure**: Walk alongside lions under the guidance of trained professionals. Learn about lion behavior and conservation efforts.

- **Safety**: Strict safety protocols ensure both visitor and animal well-being.
- **Duration**: 1–2 hours.

3. Birdwatching Tours

- **Best Times**: Early morning or late afternoon.
- **Popular Species**: African fish eagle, hornbills, and Senegal parrots.

4. Forest Walks

- **Eco-Trails**: Explore the lush woodlands of the reserve on foot with a guide. This activity offers a chance to appreciate the smaller details of Fathala's ecosystem, such as medicinal plants and smaller mammals.

Dining Options at Fathala

1. On-Site Restaurant

- **Menu**: A blend of Senegalese and international dishes featuring fresh, locally sourced ingredients.
- **Specialties**: Grilled fish, peanut-based stews, and tropical fruit desserts.
- **Opening Hours**: 7:00 AM - 10:00 PM.

2. Picnic Areas

- Visitors can enjoy a self-packed picnic in designated areas within the reserve.

Accommodation Options

For those looking to extend their visit, Fathala Wildlife Reserve offers comfortable and eco-conscious accommodation.

1. Fathala Lodge
   - **Features**: Luxury tented lodges with en-suite bathrooms, private decks, and views of the surrounding wilderness.
   - **Amenities**: Swimming pool, on-site bar, and guided activities.
   - **Pricing**: From XOF 100,000 per night.
2. Budget Accommodation Nearby
   - **Campements Villageois** in Karang or Kaolack offer simpler lodging options for budget travelers, starting at XOF 15,000 per night.

Best Time to Visit

The dry season (November to May) is ideal for visiting Fathala Wildlife Reserve. The weather is cooler, and animals are more visible near watering holes.

Tips for Visiting Fathala Wildlife Reserve

1. **What to Bring**:
   - Comfortable, lightweight clothing in neutral colors.
   - Binoculars for birdwatching.
   - Sunscreen and insect repellent.
2. **Booking Activities**:
   - Book guided tours and lion walks in advance, especially during peak seasons.
3. **Respect Wildlife**:
   - Keep a safe distance from animals and follow guide instructions.

- o Avoid feeding or touching animals unless part of a supervised activity.

Nearby Attractions

Fathala Wildlife Reserve is conveniently located near other must-visit destinations:

- **Delta du Saloum National Park** (30 km): A UNESCO World Heritage site featuring mangroves, lagoons, and diverse marine life.
- **Kaolack Market** (50 km): One of Senegal's largest markets, offering traditional crafts, textiles, and local delicacies.

Baobab Forests and Sacred Trees

The **baobab tree**, often called the "Tree of Life," is one of Senegal's most iconic natural symbols. These majestic giants, with their massive trunks and distinctive silhouettes, hold immense ecological, cultural, and spiritual significance. Exploring Senegal's baobab forests and sacred trees offers a journey into the heart of its biodiversity and traditions.

Key Information

- **Top Baobab Locations in Senegal:**
    1. **Baobab Forest of Nguekokh**
        - **Address**: Near the village of Nguekokh, approximately 85 km southeast of Dakar.
        - **Opening Hours**: Open year-round; best visited between 7:00 AM and 5:30 PM.
        - **Pricing**: Guided tours available for XOF 2,000 - XOF 5,000 per person.

2. **Sacred Baobab of Sindia**
    - **Address**: Sindia, on the Dakar-Mbour road (N1).
    - **Opening Hours**: Daily, 8:00 AM to 6:00 PM.
    - **Pricing**: Contributions to local guides start at XOF 1,500.
3. **Bandia Wildlife Reserve**
    - **Address**: Route de Mbour, 65 km from Dakar.
    - **Opening Hours**: Daily, 8:00 AM to 5:00 PM.
    - **Pricing**: Entrance fees range from XOF 10,000 - XOF 12,000 for adults. Guided safari tours cost extra.
- **Recommended Nearby Dining**:
    - **Le Baobab Restaurant (Bandia Reserve)**:
        - **Specialties**: Grilled meats, traditional Senegalese dishes.
        - **Pricing**: XOF 4,000 - XOF 10,000.
        - **Opening Hours**: Daily, 11:00 AM - 9:00 PM.
- **Accommodation Options**:
    - **Lodge des Collines de Niassam (Palmarin)**
        - **Pricing**: From XOF 50,000 per night.
        - **Features**: Unique baobab-view chalets.

The Majesty of the Baobab Tree

Ecological Significance

- **Adaptation to Arid Environments**: Baobabs store water in their massive trunks, enabling survival in Senegal's dry climate.

- **Biodiversity Hotspots**: Baobab forests support diverse ecosystems, providing food and shelter for birds, monkeys, and insects.

Unique Features

- Baobabs can live for over 1,000 years, with some specimens in Senegal believed to be 2,000 years old.
- The trees bear a nutrient-rich fruit known as **pain de singe** (monkey bread), consumed locally and exported globally for its health benefits.

Sacred Trees and Spiritual Connections

Cultural Importance

Baobabs are deeply intertwined with Senegalese culture and spirituality. They are often associated with ancestral spirits and serve as meeting places for ceremonies and storytelling.

- **Sacred Baobabs**: Certain trees, such as the **Baobab of Sindia**, are revered as sacred sites where rituals and offerings take place.
- **Burial Sites**: In the past, some baobabs were used as burial sites for griots (traditional storytellers) due to their spiritual significance.

Rituals and Practices

- Visitors are often advised to approach sacred baobabs with respect, refraining from touching them without permission.
- Offerings like kola nuts or milk may be left at the base of sacred trees.

Activities in Baobab Forests

Guided Walks and Forest Exploration

- Explore the **Baobab Forest of Nguekokh** with local guides who share fascinating stories about the trees' history and ecological role.
- Duration: Half-day tours are popular, costing around XOF 3,000 per person.

Climbing and Adventure Activities

- Some trees, such as those in Bandia Reserve, offer opportunities for climbing or exploring hollow trunks.
- Adventure parks like **Accrobaobab Adventure** in Sindia feature ziplining and climbing activities around ancient baobabs.
  - **Pricing**: XOF 7,000 - XOF 15,000 per activity.

Conservation Efforts

Threats to Baobabs

- **Deforestation**: Agriculture and urbanization pose significant threats.
- **Climate Change**: Prolonged droughts and temperature changes affect baobab growth and survival.

Conservation Projects

- Organizations like **Nature Sénégal** and local communities actively work to preserve baobab forests.
- Visitors can contribute by participating in reforestation programs or donating to conservation initiatives.

Dining Under Baobabs

Dining beneath the sprawling branches of a baobab tree is a magical experience.

- **Eco-Dining Experiences**: Some lodges and restaurants, like those in the Sine-Saloum Delta, offer meals served under baobabs with a focus on traditional Senegalese cuisine.
- **Signature Dishes**:
    - Grilled fish marinated in baobab fruit juice.
    - Baobab leaf soup, known for its nutritional value.

Cultural Experiences Around Baobabs

Storytelling Evenings

- Gather around a sacred baobab as griots recount tales of Senegal's history and legends.
- Locations: Mar Lodj and Sindia villages frequently host storytelling sessions.
- Cost: Voluntary contributions of XOF 1,000 - XOF 3,000 per attendee.

Traditional Medicine

- Baobab leaves, bark, and fruit are used in local remedies for ailments like fever, digestive issues, and skin conditions.

Visiting Baobabs with Children

Baobab forests offer family-friendly activities, making them an excellent choice for travelers with children.

- **Interactive Tours**: Guides often tailor tours to engage young visitors, including climbing activities and educational talks.

- **Craft Workshops**: Some villages near baobab forests host workshops where children can learn to create traditional crafts using baobab materials.

Tips for Exploring Baobab Forests

1. **Pack Essentials**: Comfortable walking shoes, sunscreen, and plenty of water are must-haves for exploring baobab areas.
2. **Hire Local Guides**: They provide in-depth knowledge and help navigate less accessible areas.
3. **Respect Nature**: Avoid picking leaves or fruit without permission, as they are often vital to local communities.

Best Time to Visit

- **Dry Season (November to May)**: Ideal for walking tours and forest explorations.
- **Rainy Season (June to October)**: Lush greenery enhances the scenery, though some trails may become muddy.

Beaches and Coastal Escapes

Top Beaches and Coastal Destinations

1. Dakar's Beaches

Dakar, Senegal's capital, boasts several beaches that offer diverse experiences, from lively urban shores to tranquil bays.

Plage de Ngor

- **Address**: Ngor Village, Dakar.
- **Opening Times**: Open 24/7. Best visited during daylight hours.
- **Pricing**: Free access; optional boat rides to Ngor Island cost XOF 1,000 - XOF 3,000.

- **Highlights**: Calm waters, perfect for swimming and paddleboarding. The nearby Ngor Island offers secluded beaches and fresh seafood restaurants.

Plage de Yoff

- **Address**: Yoff, Dakar.
- **Opening Times**: Open 24/7. Lifeguards are present during peak hours (10:00 AM - 6:00 PM).
- **Pricing**: Free access.
- **Highlights**: A vast expanse of sand, popular with locals for football and evening strolls. Ideal for kite surfing due to strong winds.

Plage des Mamelles

- **Address**: Near Les Mamelles Lighthouse, Dakar.
- **Opening Times**: Open 24/7.
- **Pricing**: Free access.
- **Highlights**: A hidden gem with a bohemian vibe. Small beach bars serve drinks and grilled fish.

---

2. Petite Côte: A Coastal Paradise

The Petite Côte is a stretch of coastline south of Dakar, renowned for its idyllic beaches, fishing villages, and resorts.

Saly

- **Address**: Saly Portudal, Mbour District.
- **Opening Times**: Open 24/7.
- **Pricing**: Free beach access. Resort day passes start at XOF 5,000.
- **Highlights**: Senegal's most famous resort town. Offers upscale accommodations, water sports, and vibrant nightlife.

151

Popenguine Beach

- **Address**: Popenguine Village, 70 km from Dakar.
- **Opening Times**: Open 24/7.
- **Pricing**: Free access.
- **Highlights**: A peaceful retreat with golden sands, backed by cliffs and lush vegetation. Explore the Popenguine Nature Reserve for hiking and birdwatching.

Somone Lagoon and Beach

- **Address**: Somone, 77 km from Dakar.
- **Opening Times**: Open 24/7. Boat tours: 8:00 AM - 5:00 PM.
- **Pricing**: Free beach access; lagoon boat tours cost XOF 3,000 - XOF 7,000 per person.
- **Highlights**: A tranquil spot for swimming and kayaking. The nearby lagoon is home to flamingos and other bird species.

---

3. Casamance Region: Untouched Beauty

The Casamance region in southern Senegal is famed for its unspoiled beaches and lush landscapes.

Cap Skirring

- **Address**: Cap Skirring, Ziguinchor Region.
- **Opening Times**: Open 24/7.
- **Pricing**: Free beach access; resort amenities vary in cost.
- **Highlights**: Palm-lined beaches with soft white sand. Perfect for relaxation, fishing, and enjoying fresh seafood.

Kafountine

- **Address**: Kafountine, Casamance Region.
- **Opening Times**: Open 24/7.

- **Pricing**: Free access.
- **Highlights**: A laid-back fishing village with serene beaches and vibrant local culture. Known for artisanal crafts and music festivals.

Île de Karabane

- **Address**: Off the coast of Casamance, accessible by boat from Ziguinchor.
- **Opening Times**: Boat departures from 8:00 AM to 4:00 PM.
- **Pricing**: Boat rides cost XOF 5,000 - XOF 10,000 round trip.
- **Highlights**: A historic island with a tranquil beach, colonial ruins, and opportunities for kayaking and birdwatching.

Activities to Enjoy Along Senegal's Coast

1. Water Sports and Adventure

- **Surfing**: Dakar's beaches, such as Ngor Right and Ouakam, are known for world-class waves.
- **Kitesurfing**: Yoff and Somone beaches are ideal due to their strong winds.
- **Snorkeling and Diving**: Explore underwater reefs near Ngor Island and Cap Skirring.

2. Wildlife Watching

- **Dolphin Watching**: Boat tours in Somone Lagoon or Cap Skirring offer opportunities to spot dolphins.
- **Birdwatching**: Coastal areas like the Somone Lagoon and Djoudj National Bird Sanctuary are havens for avian species.

3. Beachside Wellness

- Many resorts offer yoga sessions, spa treatments, and traditional Senegalese massage therapies with a view of the ocean.

Dining Along the Coast

1. Beachfront Restaurants

- **Chez Fatou (Ngor Beach)**: Famous for grilled prawns and cocktails. Pricing: XOF 5,000 - XOF 12,000 per dish.
- **Les Manguiers (Somone)**: Offers fresh seafood and Senegalese specialties like thieboudienne. Pricing: XOF 4,000 - XOF 10,000.

2. Street Food by the Shore

- **Dibiteries**: Enjoy grilled meat skewers on Dakar's beaches. Cost: XOF 500 - XOF 1,500.
- **Fresh Coconut Stalls**: Found on most beaches, coconuts cost around XOF 300 each.

Accommodations

1. Luxury Resorts

- **Royal Horizon Baobab (Somone)**
  - Pricing: From XOF 80,000 per night.
  - Features: All-inclusive packages, private beach access, and water sports.
- **Les Almadies (Dakar)**
  - Pricing: From XOF 120,000 per night.
  - Features: High-end amenities and proximity to urban attractions.

2. Budget-Friendly Options
- **Campement Le Niafrang (Kafountine)**
    - Pricing: XOF 10,000 - XOF 20,000 per night.
    - Features: Simple lodges with beach access and cultural activities.
- **Auberge Keur Diame (Yoff)**
    - Pricing: XOF 8,000 - XOF 15,000 per night.
    - Features: Affordable rooms, close to Yoff Beach.

When to Visit

- **Best Time**: November to May during the dry season. Ideal for beach activities, wildlife watching, and water sports.
- **Avoid**: Rainy season (June to October) as some roads and trails might be inaccessible.

Practical Tips

1. **Pack Essentials**: Sunscreen, beachwear, insect repellent, and comfortable footwear for coastal hikes.
2. **Respect Local Customs**: Dress modestly near villages and avoid public displays of affection.
3. **Hire Local Guides**: Especially in Casamance, where knowledge of the area is invaluable.

Senegal River Adventures

The **Senegal River**, stretching over 1,800 kilometers from its source in Guinea through Mali, Senegal, and Mauritania, is a vital lifeline for the region. Its serene waters and lush surroundings offer a captivating backdrop for adventure, cultural immersion, and ecological exploration.

A Senegal River adventure is an unforgettable journey into the heart of West Africa's natural beauty and heritage.

Key Information

- **Location**: The river runs through northern Senegal, with key towns like Podor, Richard-Toll, and Saint-Louis offering prime access points.
- **Address for Tours**:
  - **Saint-Louis Riverfront**: Place Faidherbe, Saint-Louis, Senegal.
  - **Podor Port**: Podor, Saint-Louis Region, Senegal.
- **Opening Times**: Most tours operate from 8:00 AM to 6:00 PM. Night cruises may be available upon request.
- **Pricing**:
  - Half-Day River Cruise: XOF 10,000–XOF 25,000 per person.
  - Full-Day Excursion: XOF 20,000–XOF 50,000, depending on inclusions.
  - Private Charters: Starting at XOF 100,000.

---

1. The Senegal River: A Journey Through History and Ecology

Cultural Significance

- The river has long been a cradle of civilizations, connecting trade routes and fostering exchanges between diverse ethnic groups such as the Fulani, Wolof, and Toucouleur.
- Its banks are dotted with historic towns like **Podor** and **Saint-Louis**, which were pivotal in colonial and pre-colonial trade.

Ecological Importance

- The river supports an array of ecosystems, including wetlands, mangroves, and savannas.
- It is a sanctuary for numerous bird species, fish, and mammals, making it a hotspot for eco-tourism.

2. Top Activities Along the Senegal River

A. Boat Cruises and Pirogue Rides

Exploring the river by boat is one of the best ways to experience its grandeur.

- **Traditional Pirogue Rides**:
  - Navigate narrow channels and mangroves in a hand-carved wooden pirogue.
  - Cost: Around XOF 10,000 per person for a two-hour tour.
- **Luxury River Cruises**:
  - Larger boats equipped with modern amenities offer leisurely journeys with stunning views of the riverbanks.
- **Recommended Operators**:
  - **Coumba Tours**: Specializes in eco-friendly pirogue tours.
  - **Ndar River Cruises**: Offers customizable luxury river tours departing from Saint-Louis.

B. Birdwatching and Wildlife Safaris

The Senegal River is a haven for bird enthusiasts.

- **Birdwatching Hotspots**:
  - **Djoudj National Bird Sanctuary**: A UNESCO World Heritage Site, home to over **1.5 million birds**, including pelicans, flamingos, and cormorants.

- **Opening Hours**: 7:00 AM – 6:00 PM.
- **Entry Fee**: XOF 5,000 per person.
  - **Langue de Barbarie National Park**: Known for its sand dunes and migratory birds.
- **Wildlife Encounters**: Spot manatees, crocodiles, and hippos in their natural habitat, especially near quieter sections of the river.

C. Exploring Historic River Towns

The Senegal River is lined with charming towns that showcase the country's rich history.

- **Saint-Louis**:
  - A UNESCO-listed island city with colonial architecture and vibrant culture.
  - Key Attractions:
    - **Faidherbe Bridge**: An engineering marvel linking the island to the mainland.
    - **Place Faidherbe Market**: Perfect for souvenirs and local crafts.
- **Podor**:
  - A quiet riverside town known for its historical fort and traditional music.
  - **Podor Fort**:
    - **Opening Hours**: Daily, 9:00 AM – 5:00 PM.
    - **Entry Fee**: XOF 2,000.
- **Richard-Toll**:
  - Famous for its sugar plantations and Moorish-inspired architecture.
  - Visit the **Maison des Esclaves** to learn about the region's history.

D. Fishing Adventures

Fishing is not only a livelihood along the Senegal River but also a popular activity for visitors.

- **Fishing Excursions**:
    - Try traditional net fishing with local guides.
    - Cost: From XOF 15,000 for a half-day experience.
- **Species to Catch**: Nile perch, catfish, and tilapia.

3. Dining Along the Senegal River

Top Restaurants

- **La Résidence (Saint-Louis)**
    - **Specialties**: Grilled fish, thieboudienne (Senegalese rice and fish dish).
    - **Pricing**: Dishes from XOF 6,000–XOF 12,000.
    - **Opening Hours**: Daily, 12:00 PM – 10:00 PM.
- **Chez Ram (Podor)**
    - **Specialties**: Freshly caught fish, served with local spices and sauces.
    - **Pricing**: XOF 4,000–XOF 8,000 per meal.
    - **Opening Hours**: 10:00 AM – 8:00 PM.

4. Accommodation Options

Luxury Stays

- **Hotel de la Poste (Saint-Louis)**
    - A historic hotel with views of the river.
    - **Pricing**: From XOF 70,000 per night.

Eco-Friendly Lodges

- **Campement Villageois Djoudj**
    - o Riverside chalets close to Djoudj National Bird Sanctuary.
    - o **Pricing**: From XOF 30,000 per night.

Budget Options

- **Auberge de Podor**
    - o Simple, clean accommodations in Podor town.
    - o **Pricing**: From XOF 10,000 per night.

---

5. Best Time to Visit

- **Dry Season (November to May):**
    - o Ideal for birdwatching and boat trips due to mild weather.
- **Rainy Season (June to October):**
    - o The river is at its fullest, and the landscape is lush, though some roads may be harder to access.

---

6. Practical Tips for a Senegal River Adventure

- **What to Pack**:
    - o Lightweight clothing, insect repellent, sunscreen, and a good pair of binoculars for birdwatching.
- **Hire a Guide**: Local guides can enhance your experience by sharing cultural insights and navigating the best spots for wildlife viewing.
- **Respect Local Customs**: Always greet locals before starting conversations, and dress modestly, especially in rural areas.

CHAPTER 7.

SENEGALESE CUISINE AND DINING

Senegalese cuisine is an explosion of flavors, textures, and aromas, deeply rooted in its rich cultural and historical tapestry. Influenced by indigenous traditions, French colonial heritage, and neighboring West African countries, Senegal's dishes are a celebration of fresh ingredients, bold spices, and communal eating. A culinary journey in Senegal is incomplete without exploring the must-try dishes, iconic flavors, and dining traditions that make its food culture truly unique.

Must-Try Dishes

1. The Heart of Senegalese Cuisine: Thieboudienne

What It Is

- Known as the **national dish of Senegal**, Thieboudienne (pronounced "cheb-oo-jen") is a one-pot rice and fish dish cooked in a rich tomato-based sauce with vegetables like cassava, carrots, and cabbage.

Where to Try It

- **Chez Loutcha, Dakar**: Famous for its authentic preparation.

- **Local Homes**: Many guesthouses offer cooking classes where travelers can learn to make Thieboudienne.

Why It's Special

- Thieboudienne is more than food; it's a symbol of Senegalese hospitality and community. Traditionally served from a communal bowl, it reflects the spirit of sharing and togetherness.

---

2. Yassa Poulet: The Iconic Chicken Dish

What It Is

- A mouthwatering dish of grilled or fried chicken marinated in a tangy blend of mustard, lemon, onions, and spices, served with rice.

Where to Try It

- **Le Djolof, Dakar**: Known for its smoky and perfectly seasoned Yassa Poulet.
- **La Résidence, Saint-Louis**: Combines modern techniques with traditional flavors.

Why It's Special

- The onions are slow-cooked to create a caramelized, deeply flavorful sauce. Variants include **Yassa Poisson** (fish) and **Yassa Mouton** (lamb).

---

3. Mafé: The Peanut Stew

What It Is

- A hearty stew made with a base of ground peanuts, tomatoes, and spices, often cooked with beef, lamb, or chicken. Served with rice, it's a comforting and filling meal.

Where to Try It

- **Chez Fatou, Saint-Louis**: Offers an authentic home-style version.
- **Village Kitchens in Casamance**: Enjoy a rustic take on this dish in a traditional setting.

Why It's Special

- Mafé's creamy texture and nutty flavor make it a favorite comfort food, especially during family gatherings.

4. Street Food Staples

A. Pastels

- **What It Is**: Small, fried pastries filled with spiced fish or meat. Often served with a tangy tomato dipping sauce.
- **Where to Try It**:
    - **Sandaga Market, Dakar**: Freshly made by local vendors.
    - **Street Stalls in Saint-Louis**: Affordable and delicious.

B. Accara

- **What It Is**: Black-eyed pea fritters, crispy on the outside and soft inside.
- **Where to Try It**:
    - **Street Food Vendors in Ziguinchor**.

C. Fataya

- **What It Is**: Similar to Pastels but with more diverse fillings like egg or vegetables.
- **Where to Try It**:
    - **Markets in Kaolack**.

5. Fresh Seafood Delights

Grilled Fish

- Senegal's Atlantic coastline provides a bounty of fresh fish, grilled to perfection with local spices.
- **Where to Try It**:
    - ○ **Beachfront Restaurants in Mbour and Saly**.

Cebbu Yapp (Rice with Meat)

- A hearty rice dish often made with goat or lamb and a mix of vegetables.
- **Where to Try It**:
    - ○ **Casamance Lodges**: Known for their farm-to-table approach.

6. Sweet Treats and Beverages

A. Desserts

- **Lakh**: A millet-based porridge served with sweetened yogurt.
    - ○ **Where to Try It: Local Breakfast Spots Across Dakar**.
- **Thiakry**: Similar to Lakh but with the addition of raisins and spices.

B. Beverages

- **Bissap**: A hibiscus flower drink, sweet and tangy, served chilled.
- **Ataya**: A traditional tea ceremony involving three rounds of mint tea, each progressively sweeter.

Where to Enjoy Them

- **Street Cafés in Saint-Louis and Ziguinchor**: Offer authentic ataya experiences.

---

7. Vegetarian Options

Ndambé

- A hearty bean stew flavored with tomatoes and spices, often served with bread.
- **Where to Try It**: **Breakfast Stalls in Dakar**.

Vegetable Thieboudienne

- A meat-free version of the national dish, often served in eco-lodges like those in the Sine-Saloum Delta.

---

8. Dining Etiquette in Senegal

- **Eating Communally**: Meals are often shared from a single bowl. Use your right hand to eat if utensils aren't provided.
- **Timing**: Meals are leisurely, emphasizing social interaction.

---

9. Cooking Classes for Travelers

Many lodges and restaurants offer cooking classes where you can learn the secrets of Senegalese cuisine.

Recommended Classes

- **Cooking with Coumba (Dakar)**: Specializes in Thieboudienne and Yassa Poulet.
  - **Pricing**: XOF 15,000 per class.
- **Sine-Saloum Culinary Tours**: Focuses on traditional cooking methods using local ingredients.

10. Where to Stay for Food Enthusiasts

Dakar

- **Terrou-Bi Hotel**: Offers gourmet Senegalese dining.

Casamance

- **Kadiandoumagne Hotel, Ziguinchor**: Combines local flavors with luxury accommodations.

Saint-Louis

- **Hotel de la Poste**: Serves a blend of local and French-inspired dishes.

Street Food and Local Eateries

- **Main Food Hubs**:
    - **Dakar**: Street food stalls in Sandaga Market and upscale local eateries in Almadies.
    - **Saint-Louis**: Coastal specialties served in colonial-style restaurants.
    - **Ziguinchor (Casamance Region)**: Renowned for fresh seafood and Jola-inspired dishes.
- **Opening Hours**:
    - Street food stalls: Typically 11:00 AM to late evening (around 10:00 PM).
    - Local eateries: 12:00 PM – 3:00 PM (lunch) and 7:00 PM – 10:00 PM (dinner).
- **Pricing**:
    - Street food: XOF 500–XOF 2,000 per item.
    - Local eateries: XOF 3,000–XOF 10,000 per meal.

1. The Essence of Senegalese Cuisine

Staple Ingredients

- **Rice and Millet**: The foundation of many dishes, particularly thieboudienne.
- **Fish**: Abundant along the coast and rivers, featuring prominently in meals.
- **Spices and Herbs**: Locally sourced baobab leaves, tamarind, and bissap (hibiscus) are commonly used.
- **Peanuts**: A cornerstone of Senegalese agriculture, appearing in sauces and snacks.

Cultural Significance of Food

Food in Senegal is about more than sustenance; it's a communal experience. Meals are often shared from a single large platter, reflecting the value placed on family and community.

2. Must-Try Senegalese Street Foods

Street food is the beating heart of Senegalese gastronomy, offering affordable, flavorful, and authentic dishes.

A. Thieboudienne (Ceebu Jën)

- **What It Is**: A flavorful rice dish cooked with fish, tomatoes, vegetables, and spices.
- **Where to Try**:
  - **Sandaga Market, Dakar**
    - **Pricing**: Around XOF 1,500 per serving.
  - **Boulevard de Général de Gaulle, Saint-Louis**
    - Vendors serve home-style variations of this iconic dish.

B. Fataya

- **What It Is**: Fried pastries filled with spiced meat, fish, or vegetables.
- **Where to Try**:
  - **Soumbédioune Fish Market, Dakar**
    - **Pricing**: XOF 500 per piece.
  - **Kaolack Bus Station**: Freshly fried and served hot.

C. Accara

- **What It Is**: Deep-fried black-eyed pea fritters, often served with a spicy tomato-based dipping sauce.
- **Where to Try**:
  - **Marché HLM, Dakar**
    - **Pricing**: XOF 300–XOF 500 for a small bag.

D. Café Touba and Beignets

- **What It Is**: Spiced coffee paired with sweet, fluffy beignets (fried dough).
- **Where to Try**:
  - **Street Vendors in Saint-Louis**
    - **Pricing**: XOF 500 for coffee and beignets combo.

---

3. Local Eateries: Where Tradition Meets Modernity

For a more relaxed dining experience, Senegal's local eateries offer the perfect setting to enjoy authentic flavors with modern conveniences.

A. La Calebasse (Dakar)

- **Address**: Route des Almadies, Dakar.

- **Specialties**: Thieboudienne, yassa poulet (chicken in lemon-onion sauce).
- **Opening Hours**: 12:00 PM – 10:00 PM.
- **Pricing**: Meals from XOF 8,000.

B. Le Flamingo (Saint-Louis)
- **Address**: Quai Roume, Saint-Louis.
- **Specialties**: Grilled fish, seafood platters.
- **Opening Hours**: 12:00 PM – 3:00 PM, 7:00 PM – 10:00 PM.
- **Pricing**: Meals from XOF 6,000.

C. Chez Aissatou (Ziguinchor)
- **Address**: Boulevard 54, Ziguinchor.
- **Specialties**: Jola-style dishes like kadiokh (stewed greens).
- **Opening Hours**: 11:30 AM – 9:30 PM.
- **Pricing**: Meals from XOF 5,000.

---

4. Regional Delicacies: Beyond the Basics

Casamance Region

Known for its fertile land, this area produces unique dishes with tropical ingredients.

- **Caldou**: Fish or chicken cooked in a lime-based sauce with vegetables and served with rice.
  - **Where to Try**: Riverside eateries in Ziguinchor.

Saint-Louis

With its proximity to the sea, Saint-Louis excels in seafood.

- **Thiéré**: Couscous made from millet, served with fish or meat.
  - **Where to Try**: Colonial-style restaurants in the old town.

Eastern Senegal

The Fulani influence shines in dishes like **lakh**, a millet porridge served with sweetened yogurt or sour milk.

- **Where to Try**: Local homes in Tambacounda.

---

5. Unique Dining Experiences

A. Dakar Night Markets

- Bustling with activity, night markets offer a variety of grilled meats, fresh juices, and sweets.

B. Cooking Classes

- Participate in hands-on cooking experiences at places like **La Maison Bleue** in Dakar, where you can learn to make thieboudienne from scratch.

C. Floating Restaurants on the Senegal River

- Enjoy freshly caught fish while cruising on a traditional pirogue in Podor or Saint-Louis.

---

6. Sweet Treats and Beverages

A. Desserts

- **Thiakry**: A sweet millet pudding mixed with yogurt and sugar.
    - **Where to Try**: Traditional eateries across Dakar.
- **Ngalakh**: A peanut-based dessert with millet couscous, often served during festivals.
    - **Where to Try**: Community events or home kitchens.

B. Drinks

- **Bissap Juice**: A tangy drink made from hibiscus flowers.
- **Ginger Juice**: A zesty and refreshing beverage.

- o Both are widely available at markets for XOF 500–XOF 1,000.

---

7. Practical Tips for Enjoying Senegalese Food

- **Cultural Etiquette**: Sharing food from a communal plate is common; use your right hand for eating.
- **Hygiene**: Choose busy street food stalls for fresher and safer meals.
- **Allergies**: Inform your server of any dietary restrictions, especially regarding peanuts.

Dining Etiquette and Customs

Popular Dining Locations

- **Chez Loutcha (Dakar)**
  - o **Address**: 101 Rue Moussé Diop, Dakar, Senegal.
  - o **Opening Hours**: Daily, 11:00 AM – 11:00 PM.
  - o **Pricing**: XOF 5,000–XOF 12,000 per meal.
  - o **Specialties**: Thieboudienne, yassa poulet.
- **La Calebasse (Ngor, Dakar)**
  - o **Address**: Route de Ngor, Dakar, Senegal.
  - o **Opening Hours**: Mon–Sat, 12:00 PM – 10:30 PM.
  - o **Pricing**: XOF 7,000–XOF 15,000 per meal.
  - o **Specialties**: Grilled seafood, mafé.
- **Village des Arts Restaurant (Dakar)**
  - o **Address**: Avenue Cheikh Anta Diop, Dakar, Senegal.
  - o **Opening Hours**: Daily, 9:00 AM – 6:00 PM.
  - o **Pricing**: XOF 6,000–XOF 10,000 per meal.

- Specialties: Local snacks, vegetarian options.

Cultural Dining Experiences

- **Local Homes**: Many Senegalese families welcome visitors to share a meal, offering an authentic introduction to local dining customs.

- **Traditional Culinary Tours**:
  - **Cooking Senegal Tours**: Based in Saint-Louis, offers half-day cooking and dining experiences.
    - **Pricing**: XOF 20,000 per person.

1. Communal Dining: A Hallmark of Senegalese Culture

In Senegal, meals are more than sustenance—they are social events that foster unity and belonging. Meals are often shared communally from a single large platter, reinforcing the sense of togetherness.

The Communal Platter

- A typical Senegalese meal is served in a large bowl or platter.

- Diners gather around the platter, each person eating from the section directly in front of them.

Etiquette for Shared Meals

- **Use Your Right Hand**: It is customary to eat with the right hand, as the left hand is considered unclean in many African cultures.

- **Wait for the Elders**: Respect dictates that elders begin eating first.

- **Avoid Cross-Contamination**: Do not reach across the platter into another person's section.

2. Key Senegalese Dining Customs

Greeting Rituals

Before the meal begins, it is polite to greet everyone at the table. A simple "Nanga def?" (How are you?) or "Salaam Alaikum" (Peace be upon you) is appreciated.

Respect for Elders

Elders are highly respected in Senegalese culture. They are often served first, and diners typically seek their blessing before starting the meal.

Sharing is Caring

- Food is often seen as a communal resource, and sharing is deeply ingrained in Senegalese values.
- Guests are always encouraged to eat their fill, and refusing food may be interpreted as impolite unless there is a dietary restriction.

3. The Art of Preparing and Serving Senegalese Cuisine

Thieboudienne: The National Dish

- **Ingredients**: Fish, rice, tomatoes, and seasonal vegetables.
- **Preparation**:
    o Cooked in large pots, often over an open fire.
    o The fish is marinated in a blend of spices before being fried or stewed.

Presentation

- Dishes like thieboudienne are beautifully arranged, with the fish at the center and vegetables radiating outward, symbolizing harmony and balance.

4. Beverage Customs

Ataya: The Senegalese Tea Ceremony

- A three-round tea ceremony is a cherished tradition in Senegal. Each round is symbolic:
    - **First Cup**: Strong and bitter, representing life's challenges.
    - **Second Cup**: Sweeter, symbolizing life's joys.
    - **Third Cup**: Very sweet, reflecting friendship and community.

Bissap

- A popular hibiscus-based drink, often served chilled.
- Known for its refreshing tangy flavor, bissap pairs perfectly with spicy dishes.

5. Dining in Restaurants vs. Local Homes

Restaurants

- Urban restaurants offer a mix of traditional and international cuisines.
- Expect menus and table service.
- Tipping is not mandatory but appreciated (10% of the bill).

Home Dining

- Meals in local homes are informal but deeply ceremonial.
- Remove your shoes before entering, and express gratitude to your hosts with phrases like "Jërëjëf" (Thank you).

6. Regional Variations in Senegalese Cuisine

Dakar and Urban Centers

- Influenced by French and Middle Eastern cuisines.

175

- Popular dishes: Grilled fish, shawarma, and pastries like beignets.

Casamance Region

- Rich in tropical flavors and seafood.
- Known for dishes like **yassa poisson** (fish in onion-lemon sauce) and **bouye** (baobab fruit juice).

Northern Senegal

- Features hearty dishes like **lakh** (millet porridge with sour milk) and **couscous**.

7. Practical Tips for Dining in Senegal

- **Hydration**: Avoid tap water unless boiled or filtered. Opt for bottled or purified water.
- **Allergies**: Inform your hosts or restaurant staff in advance if you have dietary restrictions.
- **Dress Code**: While dining in homes or traditional settings, dress modestly as a sign of respect.

8. Dining Etiquette for Special Occasions

Festive Meals

During religious celebrations like **Tabaski** (Eid al-Adha) or weddings, meals are elaborate and often include lamb, rice, and sweet desserts.

Gifts for Hosts

If invited to a local home, it is thoughtful to bring a small gift, such as fruits, sweets, or a non-alcoholic beverage.

9. Noteworthy Culinary Experiences

- **Street Food Tours:**

- o Explore Dakar's bustling streets to sample local delights like **fataya** (fried pastries), **accara** (bean fritters), and **dibi** (grilled meat).
- **Cooking Classes**:
  - o Learn to prepare thieboudienne or mafé with expert chefs in Dakar or Saint-Louis.

---

10. Dining and Accommodation Pairings

Top Dining and Stay Options

- **Hotel Mermoz (Saint-Louis)**
  - o Riverfront views with a renowned seafood restaurant.
  - o Pricing: From XOF 50,000 per night.
- **Les Almadies (Dakar)**
  - o Offers gourmet Senegalese dishes and luxurious accommodations.
  - o Pricing: From XOF 75,000 per night.

Senegalese Drinks and Desserts

1. Senegalese Drinks

Drinks in Senegal are a reflection of its tropical climate, agricultural abundance, and cultural traditions. These beverages are more than thirst-quenchers—they're a window into Senegalese hospitality.

A. Bissap (Hibiscus Juice)

- **Description**: Made from dried hibiscus petals, bissap is a ruby-red, tangy, and slightly sweet drink. It is often enhanced with mint leaves, vanilla, or ginger.
- **Cultural Significance**: Known as "Senegal's national drink," bissap is served at almost every social gathering, from casual family meals to elaborate weddings.

- **Where to Try It**:
  - **Chez Loutcha, Dakar**
    - Address: 101 Rue Moussé Diop, Dakar.
    - Pricing: XOF 1,000 per glass.
  - **Street Vendors**: Especially common around Sandaga Market.

B. Bouye (Baobab Juice)

- **Description**: This creamy and slightly tangy drink is made from the pulp of the baobab fruit, known locally as the "Tree of Life." Often mixed with milk or sugar, it's both refreshing and nutritious.
- **Health Benefits**: Rich in Vitamin C and antioxidants.
- **Where to Try It**:
  - **Le Baobab, Saint-Louis**
    - Address: Avenue Faidherbe, Saint-Louis.
    - Pricing: XOF 1,500 per glass.

C. Ataya (Senegalese Tea)

- **Description**: A three-round tea ceremony using green tea, sugar, and mint. The first round is strong and bitter, the second milder, and the third sweet.
- **Cultural Importance**: Ataya is more than a drink—it's a social ritual where family and friends bond over conversation.
- **Where to Experience It**:
  - Home visits in rural areas, particularly in **Sine-Saloum Delta** villages.

D. Ginger Juice (Jus de Gingembre)

- **Description**: A spicy and invigorating drink made by blending fresh ginger with lemon juice and sugar.

- **Occasions**: Often served as a palate cleanser or to energize during hot afternoons.
- **Where to Try It**:
  - **Ngor Café, Dakar**
    - Address: Plage de Ngor, Dakar.
    - Pricing: XOF 1,200 per glass.

E. Palm Wine (Sodabi)

- **Description**: A naturally fermented drink made from palm sap. It is slightly alcoholic and has a distinct sweet and sour flavor.
- **Occasions**: Consumed mostly during traditional ceremonies and celebrations.
- **Where to Try It**:
  - Local villages in the **Casamance region**.

---

2. Senegalese Desserts

Senegalese desserts are a delightful fusion of local ingredients, French influence, and African culinary traditions.

A. Thiakry (Millet Pudding)

- **Description**: A creamy dessert made from millet grains, mixed with sweetened yogurt, milk, and flavored with nutmeg or vanilla.
- **Cultural Importance**: Thiakry is often served during Ramadan or as a sweet treat at family gatherings.
- **Where to Try It**:
  - **La Calebasse, Dakar**
    - Address: Route des Almadies, Dakar.
    - Pricing: XOF 2,500 per serving.

B. Pastels Sucrés (Sweet Pastels)

- **Description**: Fried dough pockets filled with sweetened coconut or peanuts.
- **Where to Try It**:
  - Sandaga Market stalls in Dakar.
  - Pricing: XOF 500–XOF 1,000 per pastel.

C. Banana Fritters (Beignets de Banane)

- **Description**: Fried banana dough balls served with a dusting of sugar or honey.
- **Where to Try It**:
  - **Linguère Café, Saint-Louis**
    - Address: Quai Roume, Saint-Louis.
    - Pricing: XOF 1,500 per portion.

D. Dégué

- **Description**: A sweetened couscous dish combined with yogurt, milk, and sugar. Often served chilled.
- **Where to Try It**:
  - Street vendors across Dakar and Saint-Louis.

E. Sombi (Rice Pudding)

- **Description**: A creamy rice dessert cooked with coconut milk, sugar, and sometimes spiced with cinnamon.
- **Where to Try It**:
  - **La Kora, Gorée Island**
    - Address: Rue des Esclaves, Gorée.
    - Pricing: XOF 2,000 per serving.

3. Signature Dining Experiences

Le Lodge des Almadies

- **Specialties**: Offers a dessert platter featuring thiakry, sombi, and banana fritters.
- **Address**: Route de Ngor, Almadies, Dakar.
- **Pricing**: Dessert platter from XOF 6,000.

L'Île Gourmande

- **Specialties**: Bissap sorbet and baobab ice cream.
- **Address**: Gorée Island, Dakar.
- **Pricing**: Ice cream from XOF 3,500.

---

4. Desserts for the Adventurous Palate

If you're feeling adventurous, try desserts that incorporate exotic Senegalese ingredients like tamarind or kinkeliba (a local herbal tea). These flavors offer a unique twist to traditional recipes.

---

5. Pairing Drinks with Desserts

Pairing Senegalese drinks and desserts can elevate your culinary experience.

- **Bissap with Thiakry**: The tanginess of bissap complements the creamy sweetness of thiakry.
- **Baobab Juice with Sombi**: The tart flavor of bouye balances the rich coconut flavor of rice pudding.
- **Ataya with Banana Fritters**: The strong tea flavor contrasts beautifully with the sweetness of the fritters.

---

6. Seasonal Availability

Many of Senegal's fruits and ingredients are seasonal, so drinks and desserts might vary throughout the year. Mangoes, papayas, and baobab are more abundant during the rainy season (June–October), influencing the flavors you'll encounter.

---

7. Tips for Enjoying Senegalese Drinks and Desserts

- **Embrace the Rituals**: For drinks like ataya, take your time to savor the ceremonial preparation and social atmosphere.

- **Street Food Hygiene**: Choose vendors with high turnover for the freshest and safest treats.

- **Experiment**: Don't hesitate to try fusion desserts, like bissap-flavored ice cream or baobab cheesecake, which are becoming popular in urban cafes.

CHAPTER 8.

ACCOMMODATIONS IN SENEGAL

Senegal offers a wealth of high-end accommodations that blend luxury, comfort, and cultural immersion. Whether you're seeking beachfront opulence, urban sophistication, or eco-friendly luxury amidst natural landscapes, Senegal's luxury resorts and hotels cater to every preference. This guide provides comprehensive insights into the top luxury accommodations across Senegal, including addresses, amenities, pricing, dining options, and nearby attractions.

Luxury Resorts and Hotels

1. The King Fahd Palace Hotel

- **Location**: Route des Almadies, Dakar.
- **Opening Hours**: 24/7.
- **Pricing**: Starting at XOF 120,000 per night for standard rooms; luxury suites from XOF 300,000.
- **Contact**: +221 33 869 69 69.

Overview

The King Fahd Palace Hotel is a landmark of luxury in Dakar, offering panoramic views of the Atlantic Ocean. Renowned for its spacious rooms and suites, it caters to business travelers and leisure tourists alike.

Amenities

- 374 rooms, including ocean-facing suites.
- Olympic-sized swimming pool.
- Tennis courts and an 18-hole golf course.
- Spa and wellness center offering traditional Senegalese treatments.
- On-site fine-dining restaurants serving international and local cuisine.

Dining Options

- **Le Manguier**: Specializes in Senegalese dishes, including yassa and thieboudienne.
- **Le Brasserie**: A French-style bistro with a curated wine list.

Nearby Attractions

- Ngor Island (10-minute drive).
- African Renaissance Monument (15-minute drive).

---

2. Royal Horizon Baobab

- **Location**: Somone Lagoon, Petite Côte.
- **Opening Hours**: 24/7.
- **Pricing**: Starting at XOF 90,000 per night for standard rooms; private bungalows from XOF 180,000.
- **Contact**: +221 33 957 57 57.

Overview

Nestled along the shores of Somone Lagoon, this resort offers unparalleled tranquility and natural beauty. The property features bungalows set amidst baobab trees and direct beach access.

Amenities

- Private beach access with sun loungers and cabanas.
- All-inclusive packages available.
- Water sports, including kayaking and paddleboarding.
- On-site cultural evenings featuring Senegalese music and dance.

Dining Options

- Buffet-style restaurant with a rotating menu of international and African dishes.
- Poolside bar serving cocktails and light snacks.

Nearby Attractions

- Bandia Wildlife Reserve (30-minute drive).
- Mbour fishing village (20-minute drive).

3. Lamantin Beach Resort & Spa

- **Location**: Saly Portudal, Petite Côte.
- **Opening Hours**: 24/7.
- **Pricing**: Starting at XOF 110,000 per night for garden-view rooms; beachfront villas from XOF 250,000.
- **Contact**: +221 33 957 09 09.

Overview

Lamantin Beach Resort combines Senegalese architecture with modern luxury. It's a favorite among honeymooners and families seeking a mix of relaxation and adventure.

Amenities

- 145 rooms and suites with private terraces.
- Marina with yacht rentals.

- Fully-equipped spa with hammam and massage treatments.
- Kids' club and babysitting services.

Dining Options

- **Le Beach Club**: Seafood-focused menu with fresh catches daily.
- **Le Teranga**: An à la carte restaurant offering a fusion of Senegalese and Mediterranean cuisines.

Nearby Attractions

- Saly Golf Club (5-minute drive).
- Popenguine Nature Reserve (30-minute drive).

---

4. Lodge des Collines de Niassam

- **Location**: Palmarin, Sine-Saloum Delta.
- **Opening Hours**: 24/7.
- **Pricing**: Starting at XOF 75,000 per night for eco-lodges; treetop rooms from XOF 120,000.
- **Contact**: +221 77 644 20 20.

Overview

For eco-conscious travelers, this unique lodge offers accommodations in treehouses and stilted cabins overlooking lagoons and mangroves.

Amenities

- Guided canoe tours of the Sine-Saloum Delta.
- Solar-powered facilities.
- Bird-watching expeditions.
- Sunset cruises.

Dining Options

- Restaurant featuring locally sourced ingredients, including freshly caught fish and seasonal produce.

Nearby Attractions

- Fadiouth Shell Island (45-minute drive).
- Joal-Fadiouth (historical village, 1-hour drive).

---

5. Radisson Blu Hotel, Dakar Sea Plaza

- **Location**: Route de la Corniche Ouest, Dakar.
- **Opening Hours**: 24/7.
- **Pricing**: Starting at XOF 150,000 per night for standard rooms; luxury suites from XOF 400,000.
- **Contact**: +221 33 869 33 33.

Overview

A modern and sophisticated hotel located in Dakar's Corniche district, offering breathtaking views of the Atlantic Ocean.

Amenities

- Infinity pool overlooking the ocean.
- High-end shopping arcade within the property.
- Fully-equipped fitness center.
- Conference facilities for business events.

Dining Options

- **Filini Restaurant**: Specializing in Italian cuisine with a Senegalese twist.
- **Poolside Grill**: Offers fresh seafood and grilled meats.

Nearby Attractions

- Place du Souvenir Africain (5-minute walk).
- IFAN Museum of African Arts (10-minute drive).

---

6. Keur Bamboung Eco-Lodge

- **Location**: Saloum Delta Biosphere Reserve.
- **Opening Hours**: 24/7.
- **Pricing**: Starting at XOF 50,000 per night for eco-friendly lodges.
- **Contact**: +221 77 455 45 45.

Overview

This award-winning eco-lodge is designed for travelers who wish to immerse themselves in nature without sacrificing comfort.

Amenities

- Solar-powered accommodations.
- Guided eco-tours of mangroves and local villages.
- Workshops on sustainable fishing practices.

Dining Options

- Organic menu featuring baobab fruit, fresh fish, and millet dishes.

Nearby Attractions

- Palmarin Mangroves.
- Traditional fishing villages.

---

7. Hotel Mermoz

- **Location**: Saint-Louis Island.
- **Opening Hours**: 24/7.
- **Pricing**: Starting at XOF 60,000 per night.
- **Contact**: +221 33 961 36 36.

Overview

Located along the banks of the Senegal River, Hotel Mermoz is a charming retreat that combines colonial history with modern amenities.

Amenities

- Outdoor pool and sun terrace.
- Horse-riding excursions on the beach.
- On-site library with books on Senegalese history and culture.

Dining Options

- French and Senegalese fusion cuisine.

Nearby Attractions

- Langue de Barbarie National Park.
- Saint-Louis Old Town.

8. Resort Cap Skirring

- **Location**: Casamance region, southern Senegal.
- **Opening Hours**: 24/7.
- **Pricing**: Starting at XOF 80,000 per night for standard rooms; luxury villas from XOF 200,000.
- **Contact**: +221 33 990 50 50.

Overview

This resort is a haven for beach lovers, featuring pristine stretches of sand and lush greenery.

Amenities

- Golf course overlooking the ocean.
- Beachfront yoga sessions.
- Traditional Casamance-style bungalows.

Dining Options

- Local seafood specialties, including oysters and prawns.

Nearby Attractions

- Basse Casamance National Park.
- Kafountine village.

Budget-Friendly Options

1. Budget Accommodations in Dakar

A. ViaVia Dakar

- **Description**: A vibrant and traveler-friendly hostel located near the bustling Plateau district, perfect for those looking to explore Dakar on a budget.
- **Address**: Avenue Abdoulaye Fadiga, Dakar.
- **Price**: Dorm beds from XOF 6,000; private rooms from XOF 15,000 per night.
- **Facilities**: Free Wi-Fi, shared kitchen, on-site café serving local and international dishes.
- **Highlights**: Walking distance to major landmarks like the IFAN Museum and the Presidential Palace.

B. Yoff Ocean View Guesthouse

- **Description**: A cozy guesthouse with sea views, ideal for budget-conscious travelers seeking tranquility away from the city center.
- **Address**: Yoff Beach, Dakar.
- **Price**: Private rooms starting at XOF 12,000 per night.
- **Facilities**: Beach access, basic kitchen, and rooftop terrace.
- **Highlights**: Proximity to Ngor Island and Dakar Airport.

C. Auberge Keur Diame

- **Description**: A homely auberge offering budget rooms in a welcoming Senegalese setting.
- **Address**: Route de Ngor, Dakar.
- **Price**: Single rooms from XOF 8,000 per night.
- **Facilities**: Shared bathrooms, garden seating, and local meal options.
- **Highlights**: Hosts organize cultural experiences like drumming workshops.

---

2. Affordable Stays in Saint-Louis

A. La Maison Rose

- **Description**: A colonial-era guesthouse with charming décor and a welcoming atmosphere.
- **Address**: Quai Roume, Saint-Louis Island.
- **Price**: Double rooms from XOF 18,000 per night.
- **Facilities**: Free breakfast, Wi-Fi, and a communal courtyard.
- **Highlights**: Located near the Faidherbe Bridge and the bustling fish market.

B. Zebrabar Lodge

- **Description**: A tranquil eco-lodge nestled within the Langue de Barbarie National Park.
- **Address**: Langue de Barbarie, 18 km south of Saint-Louis.
- **Price**: Rustic cabins from XOF 12,000 per night.
- **Facilities**: On-site restaurant, canoe rentals, and birdwatching tours.

- **Highlights**: Perfect for nature lovers looking to explore the surrounding wetlands.

---

3. Eco-Lodges and Guesthouses in Sine-Saloum Delta

A. Keur Bamboung Eco-Lodge

- **Description**: A community-based eco-lodge set on a mangrove-filled island, promoting sustainable tourism.
- **Address**: Foundiougne, Sine-Saloum Delta.
- **Price**: Bungalows starting at XOF 14,000 per night.
- **Facilities**: Solar-powered lighting, on-site dining serving fresh seafood, and guided pirogue tours.
- **Highlights**: A peaceful retreat with opportunities for birdwatching and canoeing.

B. Ecolodge de Palmarin

- **Description**: A serene eco-lodge offering budget-friendly accommodations with a focus on environmental preservation.
- **Address**: Palmarin, Sine-Saloum Delta.
- **Price**: Rooms starting at XOF 16,000 per night.
- **Facilities**: Solar energy, natural pools, and organized cultural excursions.
- **Highlights**: Located near pristine beaches and mangrove forests.

---

4. Rustic Stays in Casamance

A. Casa Rosa Bungalow

- **Description**: A simple yet comfortable bungalow-style lodge surrounded by lush greenery.

- **Address**: Cap Skirring, Casamance.
- **Price**: Rooms from XOF 10,000 per night.
- **Facilities**: Hammocks, shared kitchen, and bicycle rentals.
- **Highlights**: Close to Cap Skirring's sandy beaches.

B. Le Kasaï

- **Description**: A budget-friendly community guesthouse offering authentic experiences.
- **Address**: Ziguinchor, Casamance.
- **Price**: Single rooms from XOF 8,000 per night.
- **Facilities**: On-site café and guides available for exploring the region.
- **Highlights**: Immersive cultural activities with local communities.

---

5. Community-Based Tourism Options

Senegal's emphasis on community-based tourism offers unique and budget-friendly stays. These accommodations are often managed by local families or cooperatives, ensuring an authentic experience while supporting the local economy.

Examples:

- **Village Stays in Joal-Fadiouth**: Experience life in Senegal's famous shell island village.
- **Campement Touristique in Kedougou**: Affordable lodges in the southeastern region, perfect for exploring Niokolo-Koba National Park.

---

6. Tips for Budget Travelers

- **Advance Booking**: Popular budget accommodations fill up quickly, especially in peak tourist seasons (November to April).
- **Shared Facilities**: Opt for hostels or auberges with shared bathrooms and kitchens to save costs.
- **Group Travel**: Splitting costs with fellow travelers can make private lodges or guesthouses more affordable.
- **Cultural Exchange**: Engage with locals to discover hidden gems and budget-friendly stays not widely advertised.

---

7. Dining and Activities at Budget Accommodations

Many budget accommodations in Senegal offer in-house dining and affordable activities:

- **Meals**: Traditional Senegalese dishes like thieboudienne or yassa are commonly offered at budget stays, costing around XOF 2,000–XOF 5,000.
- **Activities**: Hosts often organize affordable excursions like mangrove tours, cultural workshops, or visits to nearby markets.

Unique Stays: Lodges, Camps, and Guesthouses

1. Sine-Saloum Delta: Embracing Nature

The Sine-Saloum Delta is a UNESCO World Heritage Site and a haven for nature lovers. This area is famous for its mangroves, saltwater lagoons, and biodiversity.

A. Lodge des Collines de Niassam

- **Description**: Perched on stilts over a lagoon, this eco-lodge offers a blend of rustic charm and modern comfort. Guests can enjoy birdwatching and canoeing right from their doorstep.
- **Address**: Palmarin, Sine-Saloum Delta.
- **Pricing**: XOF 30,000–XOF 70,000 per night.
- **Amenities**: Private balconies, guided nature tours, and local cuisine.

B. Keur Bamboung

- **Description**: Situated in a serene mangrove forest, this community-run lodge promotes sustainable tourism. Guests stay in traditional-style huts and can explore nearby fishing villages.
- **Address**: Toubacouta, Sine-Saloum Delta.
- **Pricing**: XOF 15,000–XOF 35,000 per night.
- **Unique Features**: Solar-powered facilities and locally sourced meals.

2. Saint-Louis: Colonial Charm

Saint-Louis, Senegal's former colonial capital, is rich in history and architecture. Accommodations here are typically housed in restored colonial buildings.

A. Hôtel de la Résidence

- **Description**: This charming guesthouse is a restored colonial-era building with elegant décor and a tranquil courtyard.
- **Address**: Rue Blaise Diagne, Saint-Louis.
- **Pricing**: XOF 25,000–XOF 50,000 per night.
- **Highlights**: Proximity to Saint-Louis' lively markets and cultural sites.

B. Maison Rose

- **Description**: A boutique hotel blending French colonial architecture with contemporary art. Each room is uniquely designed, making it a favorite among creative travelers.
- **Address**: Quai Roume, Saint-Louis.
- **Pricing**: XOF 40,000–XOF 80,000 per night.
- **Dining Options**: Offers a rooftop restaurant serving fusion cuisine.

---

3. Dakar and Gorée Island: Artistic Flair

The bustling capital Dakar and its historic neighbor, Gorée Island, are known for their vibrant arts scene and cultural significance.

A. Villa Castel

- **Description**: This boutique hotel in Dakar combines contemporary design with traditional Senegalese art. The property features a lush garden and an art gallery.
- **Address**: Rue de l'Océan, Almadies, Dakar.
- **Pricing**: XOF 60,000–XOF 120,000 per night.
- **Amenities**: Pool, curated art exhibits, and gourmet dining.

B. Maison Augustin Ly

- **Description**: Located on Gorée Island, this historic house has been converted into a charming guesthouse. It offers breathtaking views of the ocean and a serene ambiance.
- **Address**: Rue de l'Escale, Gorée Island.
- **Pricing**: XOF 20,000–XOF 50,000 per night.
- **Experience**: Guests can explore Gorée's museums and colonial landmarks just steps away.

---

4. Casamance Region: Off-the-Beaten-Path

Casamance, located in southern Senegal, is known for its lush landscapes and distinctive Diola culture.

A. Les Palétuviers

- **Description**: A luxury eco-lodge nestled in a mangrove forest. Accommodations include treehouses and overwater bungalows.
- **Address**: Cap Skirring, Casamance.
- **Pricing**: XOF 50,000–XOF 150,000 per night.
- **Activities**: Kayaking, fishing, and cultural tours of Diola villages.

B. Ecolodge Kachikally

- **Description**: This rustic lodge features traditional African architecture and offers an immersive experience into local life.
- **Address**: Ziguinchor, Casamance.
- **Pricing**: XOF 20,000–XOF 40,000 per night.
- **Special Features**: Organic farming workshops and live music evenings.

---

5. Unique Themes and Concepts

A. Floating Hotels

- **Example**: Senegal River's floating lodges, such as **Le Bou el Mogdad**, offer cruises with comfortable onboard accommodations.

B. Desert Escapes

- In the Lompoul Desert, you'll find **Ecolodge de Lompoul**, where guests stay in luxury tents under the starry sky.
- **Pricing**: XOF 20,000–XOF 50,000 per night.

C. Artist Residencies

- Some accommodations double as artist residencies, such as **Raw Material Company** in Dakar, where guests can stay while engaging with local art projects.

6. Dining and Entertainment at Unique Stays

Many of Senegal's unique accommodations include dining options that showcase local ingredients and traditions.

- **Sine-Saloum Delta Lodges**: Fresh seafood and locally grown produce are highlights.
- **Saint-Louis Guesthouses**: French-Senegalese fusion cuisine is common.
- **Casamance Ecolodges**: Offer dishes made with local staples like rice, palm oil, and cashew nuts.

Entertainment often includes traditional drumming, dance performances, or storytelling sessions around a campfire.

7. Practical Tips

- **Cultural Etiquette**: Respect local customs, especially in rural areas.
- **Booking**: Contact properties directly or use trusted platforms like Jovago for seamless reservations.
- **Transportation**: Some remote stays, such as those in the Sine-Saloum Delta, may require arranging a private transfer or boat ride.

CHAPTER 9.

ADVENTURE AND ACTIVITIES

Senegal, with its diverse landscapes ranging from coastal plains to lush forests and arid savannahs, offers a wealth of hiking and trekking opportunities. Whether you're seeking a leisurely walk through picturesque villages or a challenging trek through rugged terrain, the country caters to adventurers of all levels. Here's an in-depth guide to exploring Senegal's best hiking and trekking trails.

Hiking and Trekking Trails

1. Niokolo-Koba National Park: Untamed Wilderness

Trail Highlights:

- **Address:** Kedougou region, southeastern Senegal.
- **Opening Times:** 7:00 AM–6:00 PM daily.
- **Pricing:** Park entry fee: XOF 10,000 per person. Guided treks: XOF 20,000–XOF 30,000 per group.

Niokolo-Koba National Park is Senegal's largest protected area and a UNESCO World Heritage Site. The park offers trails that take you through savannahs, wetlands, and gallery forests. Expect to encounter diverse wildlife, including antelopes, monkeys, and exotic bird species.

Recommended Trails:

- **Mount Assirik Trail:** A challenging trek that rewards hikers with panoramic views of the park's landscapes.

- **Gambia Riverbank Walk:** A moderate trail offering scenic views of the river and opportunities to spot hippos.

Tips:

- Wear lightweight but sturdy hiking boots due to uneven terrain.
- Pack binoculars for birdwatching and wildlife spotting.

---

2. Fathala Wildlife Reserve: Walking Safaris

Trail Highlights:

- **Address:** Near Karang, on the Senegal-Gambia border.
- **Opening Times:** 6:00 AM–6:00 PM.
- **Pricing:** Entry fee: XOF 5,000 per person. Guided walking safaris: XOF 15,000 per person.

Fathala Wildlife Reserve is famous for its walking safaris, offering a unique opportunity to trek among iconic African wildlife, including giraffes, zebras, and antelopes.

Unique Experience:

- **Baobab Forest Trail:** A short hike through ancient baobab trees, perfect for photography and understanding Senegal's flora.

Dining and Accommodation:

- **Nearby Lodges:** Fathala Lodge offers luxury tents starting at XOF 80,000 per night.
- **Restaurant:** On-site dining with a focus on local and international cuisine.

---

3. Baobab Forests of Sine-Saloum Delta: Iconic Landscapes

Trail Highlights:

- **Address:** Sine-Saloum Delta, central Senegal.
- **Opening Times:** 6:00 AM–6:00 PM.
- **Pricing:** Entry fee: XOF 3,000 per person. Guided hikes: XOF 10,000 per group.

This region's trails wind through stunning baobab forests, offering insight into the local ecosystem and traditional uses of baobabs in Senegalese culture.

Notable Trails:

- **Mangrove Walks:** Combine hiking with wading through shallow waters or taking a canoe ride to explore mangrove ecosystems.
- **Village Trails:** Guided treks through local villages provide cultural insights and opportunities to meet the Serer people.

---

4. Lompoul Desert: Hiking Through Golden Dunes

Trail Highlights:

- **Address:** Lompoul, located between Dakar and Saint-Louis.
- **Opening Times:** Open 24/7. Best visited during early mornings or late afternoons to avoid heat.
- **Pricing:** XOF 10,000 per guided trek.

Lompoul Desert offers a surreal trekking experience among rolling sand dunes. These treks are often combined with camel rides and overnight stays in luxury tents.

Recommended Itineraries:

- **Sunrise Hikes:** Early morning treks to witness breathtaking views of the desert illuminated by the rising sun.

- **Full-Moon Walks:** Guided nocturnal hikes under a moonlit sky create an unforgettable experience.

Accommodation and Dining:

- **Ecolodge de Lompoul:** Offers tented accommodations starting at XOF 25,000 per night, along with traditional Senegalese meals.

---

5. Casamance Region: Tropical Treks

Trail Highlights:

- **Address:** Ziguinchor and surrounding areas, southern Senegal.
- **Opening Times:** 6:00 AM–6:00 PM.
- **Pricing:** Guided hikes: XOF 15,000 per person.

Known for its lush vegetation and meandering rivers, the Casamance region offers some of Senegal's most scenic and culturally immersive hiking opportunities.

Notable Trails:

- **Diola Village Treks:** Walk through picturesque villages, learning about local customs and traditional farming practices.
- **Basse Casamance National Park:** Offers a variety of trails through dense forests with a chance to spot rare bird species.

Accommodation:

- **Ecolodge de Djembering:** Rustic yet comfortable lodges starting at XOF 20,000 per night.
- **Dining:** Fresh seafood and local dishes are served at nearby restaurants.

Essential Tips for Hiking in Senegal

1. **Gear Up:** Lightweight clothing, durable hiking boots, and hats are essential.

2. **Stay Hydrated:** Carry plenty of water, especially during the dry season.

3. **Guided vs. Solo Hikes:** While some trails are easy to navigate independently, hiring a guide enhances safety and enriches your experience with local insights.

4. **Wildlife Precautions:** Maintain a respectful distance from animals, and follow your guide's instructions in wildlife reserves.

Combining Hiking with Cultural Experiences

Many trails in Senegal pass through or near traditional villages, allowing you to combine outdoor adventure with cultural exploration. Consider extending your trek with stops for:

- **Cooking demonstrations of local dishes.**
- **Storytelling sessions with village elders.**
- **Participation in traditional music or dance performances.**

Water Sports and Activities

1. Surfing

A. Almadies Peninsula

- **Description**: Known as West Africa's surf capital, Dakar's Almadies Peninsula is ideal for surfers seeking consistent waves and varied breaks.

- **Top Spot**: Ngor Right (featured in the classic surf film *The Endless Summer*).

- **Address**: Route des Almadies, Dakar.
- **Operating Times**: Year-round, with the best surfing season from November to May.
- **Pricing**:
  - Surfboard rental: XOF 5,000–XOF 10,000 per day.
  - Lessons: XOF 15,000–XOF 25,000 per session.
- **Nearby Amenities**:
  - Accommodation: **Hotel Ngor Diarama** offers beachfront access (XOF 40,000–XOF 80,000 per night).
  - Dining: **Le Ngor** serves fresh seafood and local specialties.

B. Saint-Louis

- **Description**: A quieter alternative to Dakar, Saint-Louis offers long, mellow waves perfect for beginners.
- **Top Spot**: Hydrobase Beach.
- **Address**: Langue de Barbarie, Saint-Louis.
- **Pricing**: Surf schools like **Zebrano Surf Camp** offer packages starting at XOF 50,000 for a weekend.

---

2. Kitesurfing and Windsurfing

A. Lac Rose (Pink Lake)

- **Description**: The unique setting of this saltwater lake provides ideal conditions for beginners learning kitesurfing in a scenic, wind-reliable environment.
- **Address**: Niaga Village, 30 km from Dakar.
- **Operating Times**: October to April is the peak season for winds.

- **Pricing**:
  - Kite rental: XOF 15,000 per hour.
  - Full-day lessons: XOF 30,000–XOF 50,000.
- **Accommodation**: Stay at **Ecolodge de Lac Rose** (XOF 25,000–XOF 50,000 per night).

B. Cap Skirring

- **Description**: Located in the Casamance region, Cap Skirring combines tropical beaches with steady trade winds, making it a hotspot for kitesurfers and windsurfers.
- **Pricing**:
  - Kiteboarding lessons: XOF 20,000 per session.
  - Equipment rental: XOF 10,000 per hour.

---

3. Jet Skiing and Banana Boat Rides

A. Saly-Portudal

- **Description**: Senegal's premier beach resort, Saly, offers a variety of motorized water sports, including jet skiing and banana boat rides.
- **Address**: Petite Côte, Saly-Portudal.
- **Operating Times**: Daily from 9:00 AM to 6:00 PM.
- **Pricing**:
  - Jet ski rental: XOF 30,000–XOF 50,000 per hour.
  - Banana boat rides: XOF 5,000 per person for 15 minutes.
- **Nearby Amenities**:
  - Dining: **Chez Fatou** serves fresh fish and cocktails on the beach.

- o Accommodation: **Hotel Royam** offers sea-facing bungalows (XOF 50,000–XOF 120,000 per night).

---

4. Kayaking and Canoeing

A. Sine-Saloum Delta

- **Description**: Paddle through Senegal's UNESCO-listed mangrove forests and discover serene waterways teeming with birdlife.
- **Popular Routes**:
  - o Ndangane to Mar Lodj Island.
  - o Toubacoula mangroves.
- **Address**: Sine-Saloum Delta, accessible via Kaolack.
- **Operating Times**: Sunrise to sunset.
- **Pricing**:
  - o Kayak rental: XOF 5,000 per hour.
  - o Guided tours: XOF 15,000 per person for a half-day.
- **Accommodation**: Stay at **Les Collines de Niassam** for an immersive nature experience.

B. Senegal River

- **Description**: Explore the tranquil waters of the Senegal River, with options for both guided canoe tours and independent kayaking.
- **Top Launch Point**: Podor.
- **Pricing**: XOF 10,000 per hour for kayak rentals.

---

5. Scuba Diving and Snorkeling

A. Gorée Island

- **Description**: Dive into the crystal-clear waters surrounding Gorée Island, home to coral reefs and a variety of marine species.
- **Address**: Gorée Island, Dakar.
- **Operating Times**: Best during dry season (November to May).
- **Pricing**:
  - Snorkeling gear rental: XOF 5,000 per day.
  - Diving packages: XOF 25,000–XOF 50,000.
- **Experience**: Combine diving with a cultural visit to the island's museums and historic landmarks.

B. Almadies Peninsula

- **Description**: Known for its shipwrecks and vibrant underwater ecosystems, this area attracts advanced divers.
- **Pricing**: Guided dives start at XOF 30,000 per person.

---

6. Paddleboarding and Sailing

A. Ngor Island

- **Description**: Located just off Dakar, Ngor Island offers calm waters for paddleboarding and small sailboats for hire.
- **Address**: Ngor Island, accessible by ferry from Ngor Beach.
- **Pricing**:
  - Paddleboard rental: XOF 5,000 per hour.
  - Sailing lessons: XOF 20,000 per session.

B. Cap Skirring

- **Description**: Paddleboard along the serene coastline of Cap Skirring, where the water is calm and clear.

---

7. Dining and Accommodation Near Water Sports Hubs

- **Dakar**:
  - Dining: **La Cabane du Pêcheur** serves freshly caught seafood near Ngor Beach.
  - Accommodation: **Terrou-Bi Hotel** offers luxury stays with direct beach access (XOF 80,000–XOF 200,000 per night).
- **Saly-Portudal**:
  - Dining: **Le Safari Beach** offers beachfront dining with a view.
  - Accommodation: **Lamantin Beach Resort** provides upscale accommodations (XOF 70,000–XOF 150,000 per night).

Practical Tips for Water Sports in Senegal

- **Best Season**: November to May offers calm seas and predictable winds for most water sports.
- **Safety**: Always ensure that lifejackets are provided and follow the guidance of certified instructors.
- **Booking**: Many activities can be arranged through local hotels or tour operators in advance.

9.3. Birdwatching and Safari Experiences

1. Birdwatching in Senegal: A Bird-Lover's Dream

Senegal is home to over 600 bird species, making it a premier destination for birdwatchers. Its diverse ecosystems, including wetlands, forests, savannas, and coastal regions, offer habitats to both migratory and resident birds.

A. Djoudj National Bird Sanctuary

- **Highlights**:
    - This UNESCO World Heritage Site is the third-largest bird sanctuary in the world.
    - Seasonal visitors include flamingos, pelicans, herons, and over a million migratory birds from Europe.
    - Guided boat tours allow for up-close encounters with massive flocks of pelicans during feeding time.
- **Tips**:
    - Visit between November and March for peak bird migration.
    - Bring binoculars, a telephoto lens, and a field guide to Senegalese birds.

B. Saloum Delta National Park

- **Highlights**:
    - Recognized as a biosphere reserve, this delta is a blend of mangroves, lagoons, and dry savannas.
    - Species include African fish eagles, Goliath herons, and kingfishers.
    - A sunset boat tour is particularly enchanting, with birds returning to roost in the mangroves.

C. Key Tips for Birdwatching

- **Best Gear**: Lightweight binoculars, birding guides, and comfortable walking shoes.

- **Best Time**: Early mornings and late afternoons, when birds are most active.

---

2. Safari Experiences: Exploring Senegal's Wildlife

Unlike East Africa's safari destinations, Senegal offers a more intimate and less commercialized wildlife experience. Parks and reserves are well-managed and provide opportunities to see diverse animals in their natural habitats.

A. Niokolo-Koba National Park

- **Wildlife Highlights**:
  - o Senegal's largest national park and a UNESCO World Heritage Site.
  - o Home to lions, leopards, elephants, chimpanzees, antelopes, hippos, and crocodiles.
  - o The park's rich biodiversity includes over 300 bird species and countless plant varieties.

- **Safari Options**:
  - o Guided jeep safaris, walking tours, and boat trips along the Gambia River.
  - o Multi-day safaris with overnight stays at eco-lodges within the park, such as Simenti Lodge.

B. Bandia Wildlife Reserve

- **Wildlife Highlights**:
  - o A smaller reserve with easily spotted animals, perfect for first-time safari-goers.

- Species include giraffes, zebras, buffalos, monkeys, and rhinoceroses.
  - The reserve also offers an archaeological site featuring ancient baobab trees with historical significance.
- **Safari Tips**:
  - Opt for guided tours for expert insights into the animals and ecosystems.

---

3. Unique Adventures: Beyond Traditional Safaris

A. Mangrove Kayaking in the Saloum Delta

- Explore the intricate network of mangroves by kayak. This quiet approach lets you observe wading birds, crabs, and even dolphins without disturbing their habitat.

B. Walking Safaris in Niokolo-Koba

- Accompanied by knowledgeable rangers, walking safaris allow for an immersive experience, focusing on smaller wildlife and plant life often missed in vehicle tours.

C. River Cruises on the Senegal River

- Multi-day river cruises provide a relaxing way to experience the region's wildlife and cultural sites, combining birdwatching with visits to local fishing villages.

---

4. Dining and Accommodation Options

Dining

- Many parks and reserves offer onsite restaurants serving local Senegalese dishes like *thieboudienne* (rice and fish) and *yassa* (marinated chicken or fish).

- Recommended: Bandia Reserve's onsite restaurant overlooking a watering hole.

Accommodation

1. **Djoudj National Bird Sanctuary**:
   - **Campement du Djoudj**: Basic eco-lodge close to the park entrance. Pricing starts at XOF 15,000 per night.

2. **Niokolo-Koba National Park**:
   - **Simenti Lodge**: Offers basic but comfortable accommodation with river views. Pricing starts at XOF 25,000 per night.

3. **Saloum Delta**:
   - **Ecolodge Palmarin**: Blends luxury with eco-sustainability. Pricing starts at XOF 50,000 per night.

4. **Bandia Reserve**:
   - **Nearby Hotels in Saly**: Luxurious options like Lamantin Beach Resort are available.

---

5. Practical Tips for Birdwatching and Safari Adventures

- **Clothing**: Wear neutral colors, lightweight fabrics, and comfortable footwear. Carry a hat and sunglasses for sun protection.
- **Essentials**: Bring water, sunscreen, insect repellent, and a small backpack.
- **Photography**: Use a telephoto lens for capturing wildlife from a safe distance.

9.4. Volunteering and Community Tourism

1. Sine-Saloum Delta: Sustainable and Eco-Friendly Initiatives

The Sine-Saloum Delta is a hub for eco-tourism and sustainability projects, making it ideal for those interested in environmental conservation.

A. Mangrove Restoration Projects

- **Location**: Palmarin Village, Sine-Saloum Delta.
- **Address**: Mangrove Park Office, Palmarin.
- **Opening Times**: 8:00 AM – 6:00 PM, daily.
- **Pricing**: XOF 15,000–XOF 30,000 for a week-long volunteer experience.

Participants in mangrove restoration projects help replant vital mangrove forests that combat coastal erosion and provide a habitat for local wildlife. Volunteers often stay in eco-lodges like Keur Bamboung and are guided by local experts.

B. Community Cultural Immersion

- **Focus**: Learning traditional Serer customs, such as weaving and fishing.
- **Host**: Women's Cooperative in Palmarin.
- **Cost**: XOF 20,000 per day, including meals.

Travelers can stay with local families to experience daily life, traditional cooking, and craft-making, contributing directly to community empowerment.

---

2. Casamance Region: Agricultural and Cultural Initiatives

Casamance, a lush and culturally rich region, offers opportunities to work in agriculture, education, and cultural exchange.

214

A. Organic Farming in Ziguinchor

- **Location**: Ecolodge Kachikally, Ziguinchor.
- **Address**: Route de Bambey, Ziguinchor.
- **Timing**: Programs run year-round.
- **Pricing**: XOF 25,000 per week, including accommodation and meals.

This program focuses on sustainable agriculture, teaching volunteers about local farming techniques and eco-friendly practices. The ecolodge also organizes community workshops where volunteers can assist with educational programs on health and nutrition.

B. Traditional Music and Dance Workshops

- **Host**: Diola Cultural Center, Oussouye.
- **Address**: Oussouye Main Road, Casamance.
- **Opening Times**: 10:00 AM – 5:00 PM, Monday to Saturday.
- **Cost**: XOF 5,000 per session or XOF 25,000 for a week-long course.

These workshops allow visitors to learn about Casamance's vibrant music traditions while supporting local artists. Participants can also assist in organizing performances or creating promotional materials for the center.

---

3. Dakar and Surrounding Areas: Urban Volunteering Opportunities

Dakar, as Senegal's bustling capital, has a range of projects focusing on education, healthcare, and the arts.

A. Teaching in Local Schools

- **Location**: Yoff Village, Dakar.
- **Address**: Yoff Community Center, Rue de la Paix.
- **Timing**: 8:00 AM – 3:00 PM, Monday to Friday.

- **Cost**: Typically free; donations to the school are encouraged.

Volunteers teach English, French, or basic computer skills to children and young adults. Accommodations are usually with host families, providing a close-knit community experience.

B. Art Therapy and Workshops

- **Host**: Raw Material Company, Dakar.
- **Address**: Rue Jules Ferry, Dakar.
- **Opening Times**: 9:00 AM – 6:00 PM, Monday to Saturday.
- **Cost**: XOF 10,000 per day or XOF 50,000 for a week.

Volunteers collaborate with local artists to organize workshops for underserved communities, including women and children. These programs use art as a tool for empowerment and healing.

---

4. Saint-Louis: Historical and Youth Development Projects

Saint-Louis is a UNESCO World Heritage Site and offers unique opportunities to work on heritage preservation and youth programs.

A. Restoring Colonial Architecture

- **Location**: Historic District, Saint-Louis.
- **Host**: Saint-Louis Heritage Society.
- **Timing**: Flexible schedules, depending on the project.
- **Cost**: XOF 10,000 per day.

Participants assist local artisans in restoring colonial-era buildings, learning traditional techniques and gaining insights into Senegal's architectural history.

B. Youth Sports Coaching

- **Address**: Saint-Louis Youth Center, Avenue de Gaulle.
- **Opening Times**: 9:00 AM – 4:00 PM, Monday to Friday.

- **Cost**: Free; volunteers must provide their own sports equipment.

Volunteers coach basketball, soccer, and other sports, promoting teamwork and leadership skills among local youth. This program is particularly popular with travelers looking to combine physical activity with social impact.

5. Highlights of Community Tourism

A. Home-Stay Experiences

- Staying with a host family in a rural village offers the ultimate cultural immersion. Guests learn to cook traditional dishes, participate in daily chores, and join celebrations like weddings or naming ceremonies.

B. Women's Empowerment Projects

- Many programs focus on empowering women through skill development. For example, weaving cooperatives in Thiès train volunteers in traditional techniques while creating economic opportunities for local women.

C. Wildlife and Conservation Volunteering

- Projects such as marine conservation in Joal-Fadiouth focus on protecting endangered species like sea turtles. Participants assist in patrolling beaches, monitoring nests, and educating local communities.

6. Dining and Accommodation Options

Most volunteering programs include meals and lodging, often in basic but comfortable facilities. Food typically reflects local cuisine, with dishes like *thieboudienne* (fish and rice) and fresh fruits served daily.

- **Sine-Saloum Delta**: Eco-lodges and community centers with traditional Senegalese meals.

- **Casamance**: Host families provide fresh, locally sourced meals.

- **Dakar**: Guesthouses near project sites, offering a mix of local and international dishes.

7. Practical Tips for Volunteering

- **Language**: Basic knowledge of French or Wolof is helpful, but translation assistance is often available.

- **Health**: Ensure you have all necessary vaccinations and carry basic first-aid supplies.

- **Cultural Sensitivity**: Respect local customs and dress modestly, especially in rural areas.

- **Documentation**: Bring copies of your passport and travel insurance for program registration..

CHAPTER 10.

SHOPPING AND SOUVENIRS

Senegal's markets and artisan hubs are vibrant spaces where culture, creativity, and tradition intersect. Whether you're exploring the bustling streets of Dakar or venturing into small villages, these markets offer an authentic glimpse into Senegalese life while allowing you to bring home unique, handcrafted treasures. Here's an in-depth guide to Senegal's local markets and artisans, complete with essential addresses, opening times, pricing, and insider tips

Local Markets and Artisans

1. Dakar: The Capital's Shopping Highlights

A. Sandaga Market

- **Address**: Avenue Emile Badiane, Dakar.
- **Opening Times**: 8:00 AM – 8:00 PM daily.
- **Pricing**: Prices vary, but haggling is customary. Expect to pay XOF 1,000–XOF 10,000 for smaller items, and XOF 20,000+ for larger purchases.

Sandaga is Dakar's largest and most iconic market, offering everything from traditional clothing and accessories to household goods. It's an ideal spot to buy *boubous* (traditional garments), batik fabrics, and wooden carvings. The market's maze-like alleys are best navigated with a local guide for a seamless experience.

B. Soumbedioune Artisan Village

- **Address**: Corniche Ouest, Dakar.
- **Opening Times**: 9:00 AM – 7:00 PM daily.
- **Pricing**: Jewelry starts at XOF 2,000, while larger crafts like masks and sculptures range from XOF 15,000–XOF 100,000.

This artisan hub is perfect for purchasing handcrafted jewelry, leather goods, and vibrant paintings. Artists often work on-site, offering a glimpse into their creative process. Don't miss the intricately designed silver jewelry and beaded accessories, which make for stunning keepsakes.

C. HLM Market

- **Address**: Rue HLM, Dakar.
- **Opening Times**: 9:00 AM – 6:00 PM, Monday to Saturday.
- **Pricing**: Fabric prices start at XOF 2,500 per meter; tailoring costs extra.

Known for its colorful wax print fabrics, HLM Market is a textile lover's paradise. Choose from bold, geometric patterns or more subdued floral designs. Many stalls also offer tailoring services, so you can have custom garments made on-site.

---

2. Saint-Louis: A Blend of History and Craftsmanship

A. Village des Artistes

- **Address**: Quai Roume, Saint-Louis.
- **Opening Times**: 10:00 AM – 6:00 PM, Monday to Saturday.
- **Pricing**: Artworks range from XOF 20,000–XOF 200,000, depending on the medium.

Located in the historic district, this artist village showcases the work of local painters, sculptors, and textile designers. Many pieces are inspired by Saint-Louis's colonial history and its vibrant music scene. Look out for paintings featuring jazz motifs, which reflect the city's annual jazz festival.

B. Saint-Louis Main Market

- **Address**: Rue Blaise Diagne, Saint-Louis.
- **Opening Times**: 8:00 AM – 7:00 PM daily.
- **Pricing**: Affordable, with many items priced under XOF 5,000.

This bustling market is ideal for picking up everyday items like spices, dried fish, and woven baskets. It's a sensory feast, with vendors calling out their wares and the aroma of freshly ground spices filling the air.

---

3. Casamance: Unique Souvenirs from the South

A. Ziguinchor Craft Market

- **Address**: Avenue de la Paix, Ziguinchor.
- **Opening Times**: 9:00 AM – 6:00 PM, Monday to Saturday.
- **Pricing**: Handwoven baskets start at XOF 3,000; larger carvings can cost XOF 25,000+.

Casamance is known for its distinctive crafts, including handwoven baskets, woodcarvings, and pottery. The Ziguinchor Craft Market is a great place to find these items, often crafted using traditional methods passed down through generations.

B. Diola Villages

- **Location**: Various villages near Oussouye, Casamance.
- **Timing**: Open throughout the day; visits are best arranged in the morning.
- **Pricing**: Fair-trade prices are set by the village cooperatives.

Diola villages in Casamance specialize in basketry and textiles. Purchasing directly from artisans supports community initiatives while ensuring you get a one-of-a-kind piece.

4. Sine-Saloum Delta: Eco-Friendly and Cultural Crafts

A. Foundiougne Market

- **Address**: Foundiougne Town Center.
- **Opening Times**: 8:00 AM – 4:00 PM, Tuesday and Friday.
- **Pricing**: Handmade crafts start at XOF 1,500.

Foundiougne's market focuses on eco-friendly crafts like recycled glass jewelry and raffia mats. Visitors can also find traditional musical instruments, such as *kora* (string instruments) and *djembes* (drums).

B. Joal-Fadiouth Artisan Center

- **Address**: Shell Island, Joal-Fadiouth.
- **Opening Times**: 10:00 AM – 5:00 PM daily.
- **Pricing**: Items range from XOF 2,000–XOF 10,000.

This artisan center specializes in shell-based crafts, reflecting the unique environment of Fadiouth. Items include necklaces, bracelets, and wall decor made from polished shells.

5. Kaolack: Spices and More

A. Kaolack Central Market

- **Address**: Place de l'Indépendance, Kaolack.
- **Opening Times**: 8:00 AM – 6:00 PM daily.
- **Pricing**: Spices range from XOF 500–XOF 2,000 per packet.

Known as the spice capital of Senegal, Kaolack's market is a must-visit for foodies. Pick up locally grown peanuts, hibiscus flowers, and spice blends like *thiouraye*, a fragrant mix used in Senegalese cuisine.

6. Insider Tips for Market Shopping

- **Bargaining**: Polite negotiation is expected in most markets. Start by offering half the quoted price and work your way up.

- **Language**: Learning basic Wolof phrases like "Naka nga def?" (How are you?) and "Nii mel naa ci cher bi?" (How much is this?) can enhance your shopping experience.

- **Authenticity**: To ensure you're buying authentic items, ask artisans about their techniques and materials. Avoid mass-produced items often sold near tourist hotspots.

- **Cash is King**: Many vendors do not accept credit cards, so carry enough CFA francs in smaller denominations.

7. Dining and Accommodation Near Markets

Dakar

- **Dining**: Try Chez Loutcha for authentic Senegalese cuisine near Sandaga Market.
    - **Address**: Rue Carnot, Dakar.
    - **Opening Times**: 12:00 PM – 10:00 PM.
- **Accommodation**: Stay at Novotel Dakar, located close to the city's major markets.
    - **Pricing**: Rooms start at XOF 75,000 per night.

Saint-Louis

- **Dining**: Enjoy fresh seafood at La Linguère after shopping.
    - **Address**: Quai Roume, Saint-Louis.

- **Opening Times**: 11:30 AM – 10:00 PM.
- **Accommodation**: Hotel de la Poste offers a historic ambiance and proximity to markets.
  - **Pricing**: Rooms start at XOF 50,000 per night.

Casamance

- **Dining**: Try Le Karabane for local dishes made with fresh produce.
  - **Address**: Avenue de la Paix, Ziguinchor.
  - **Opening Times**: 12:00 PM – 9:00 PM.
- **Accommodation**: Ecolodge Kachikally offers eco-friendly stays near craft markets.
  - **Pricing**: Rooms start at XOF 40,000 per night.

Authentic Senegalese Crafts

1. Fabrics and Textiles

A. Wax Prints and Batik

Senegal is renowned for its vibrant wax-printed fabrics and hand-dyed batik textiles. These fabrics are often transformed into clothing, accessories, or decorative pieces.

- **Where to Buy**:
  - Sandaga Market in Dakar is the best place to find an extensive variety of wax prints.
  - The Marché de Thiès specializes in batik fabrics with unique, hand-painted designs.
- **Tips for Buying**:
  - Look for fabrics with bold, high-quality prints.
  - Always check the stitching and dye consistency to ensure authenticity.

225

B. Woven Textiles

Handwoven textiles are a specialty in regions like Thiès. The craftsmanship reflects traditional weaving techniques passed down for generations.

- **Popular Items**:
    - Table runners, shawls, and wall hangings.
    - Prices start from XOF 7,000 for small pieces.

---

2. Jewelry

A. Beaded Jewelry

Handcrafted beaded jewelry is a staple in Senegalese markets, offering vibrant, colorful designs inspired by local traditions.

- **Where to Buy**:
    - The Village des Arts in Dakar is a top spot for original designs.
    - Casamance craft centers provide authentic Diola-style beadwork.
- **Popular Pieces**:
    - Necklaces and bracelets featuring semi-precious stones.

B. Silver and Brass Creations

Artisans in Saint-Louis are known for their exquisite silver and brass jewelry, including rings, earrings, and intricate pendants.

---

3. Wooden Crafts

A. Sculptures and Masks

Wooden masks and figurines are among the most iconic Senegalese crafts, often representing ancestral spirits or cultural symbols.

- **Where to Buy**:
    - The artisanal village in Saint-Louis and Casamance craft markets.
    - Prices range from XOF 10,000 to XOF 50,000, depending on size and detail.

B. Functional Wooden Items

Many artisans create functional yet decorative items, such as bowls, utensils, and furniture.

---

4. Leather Goods

A. Bags and Sandals

Leather crafting in Senegal is both a practical and artistic tradition, producing durable and stylish goods.

- **Where to Buy**:
    - Marché HLM in Dakar offers high-quality leather bags and sandals.

B. Decorative Pieces

Leather wall hangings and pouches make excellent souvenirs.

---

5. Pottery and Ceramics

A. Traditional Clay Pots

Pottery crafted in rural Senegalese villages often serves both decorative and functional purposes.

- **Where to Buy**:
  - Visit artisanal markets in Thiès or Casamance.

B. Decorative Ceramics

Casamance is particularly renowned for its intricately painted ceramic plates and vases.

---

6. Musical Instruments

A. Djembe Drums

The djembe is an iconic West African drum often used in Senegalese music and dance.

- **Where to Buy**:
  - Sandaga Market in Dakar and craft markets in Saint-Louis.
  - Prices range from XOF 15,000 to XOF 50,000, depending on the size and quality.

B. Kora Harps

This traditional string instrument is both a musical and decorative item.

- **Where to Buy**:
  - Specialist music shops in Dakar or artisan markets in Casamance.

---

7. Antiques and Historical Souvenirs

For collectors, Senegal offers a range of antique items, including colonial-era artifacts and traditional weaponry.

- **Where to Buy**:
  - Saint-Louis markets and upscale shops in Dakar.

- Prices can range significantly, starting at XOF 20,000.

---

8. Practical Tips for Shopping Senegalese Crafts

1. **Bargaining**:
   - Negotiating prices is customary, but always do so respectfully.

2. **Authenticity**:
   - Seek items directly from artisans or trusted markets to ensure quality.

3. **Shipping**:
   - For larger items, arrange for shipping through local vendors or courier services.

CHAPTER 11.

DAY TRIPS AND EXCURSIONS

Gorée Island

Getting to Gorée Island

The ferry from Dakar's Port de Gorée is the only way to access Gorée Island. The 20-minute journey provides stunning views of the Atlantic Ocean and the Dakar coastline. It's advisable to arrive at the ferry terminal 30 minutes early, especially during weekends or peak tourist seasons.

Exploring Gorée Island

1. Maison des Esclaves (House of Slaves)

One of the most iconic landmarks on Gorée Island, the Maison des Esclaves is a solemn reminder of the transatlantic slave trade.

- **Highlights**:
  - The *Door of No Return*: A narrow passage through which enslaved individuals were taken to ships bound for the Americas.
  - Restored holding cells: These stark, confined spaces illustrate the harsh conditions endured by captives.
  - Exhibits: Historical artifacts, photographs, and accounts of the slave trade.

230

- **Tips for Visitors**:
    - Engage with the knowledgeable guides for an in-depth understanding.
    - Photography is allowed but requires respect for the sensitive nature of the site.

2. Gorée Castle and Historical Museum

Built in the 19th century, Gorée Castle served as a colonial fortification and now houses a historical museum.

- **Highlights**:
    - Cannons and artillery from colonial times.
    - Panoramic views of Dakar's skyline and the Atlantic Ocean.
    - Exhibits detailing Senegal's history, from pre-colonial times to independence.

3. Street Art and Galleries

Gorée Island is a haven for artists, with vibrant street murals and numerous galleries showcasing Senegalese art.

- **Notable Galleries**:
    - **Galerie Arte Gorée**: Features contemporary pieces by local artists.
    - **Espace Medina**: Focuses on traditional crafts and sculptures.

4. Colonial Architecture

The island's cobblestone streets are lined with pastel-colored colonial buildings, many of which date back to the 18th and 19th centuries.

Exploring these structures provides a glimpse into Gorée's historical charm.

5. Beaches and Relaxation

While small, Gorée Island offers a few serene beach spots ideal for unwinding. The sheltered bays are perfect for swimming or sunbathing.

- **Plage de Gorée**: A small beach near the ferry terminal, popular among locals and tourists alike.
- **Snorkeling**: The clear waters around the island are home to marine life, making snorkeling a delightful activity.

Cultural Significance and Events

1. Gorée Diaspora Festival

Held annually, this event celebrates African heritage and the contributions of the diaspora to global culture.

- **Activities**:
    o Traditional music and dance performances.
    o Art exhibitions.
    o Lectures and discussions on African identity.

2. Live Music and Storytelling

Evenings on Gorée Island often come alive with live performances of traditional Senegalese music, including *kora* and *djembe*.

Dining on Gorée Island

The culinary experience on Gorée Island combines Senegalese staples with fresh seafood.

Must-Try Dishes

- **Thieboudienne**: Senegal's national dish, made with fish, rice, and vegetables.

- **Pastels**: Fried pastries filled with fish or meat, served with a spicy dipping sauce.

Tips for Visitors

1. **Wear Comfortable Shoes**: Gorée Island's cobblestone streets and uneven pathways make sturdy footwear essential.

2. **Stay Hydrated**: Carry water, especially during hot days.

3. **Respect the Environment**: Help preserve the island's charm by disposing of trash responsibly.

Bandia Wildlife Reserve

The Reserve's Highlights

1. Spectacular Wildlife

Bandia Wildlife Reserve is home to over 3,500 hectares of savannah teeming with iconic African species reintroduced to the region as part of conservation efforts. Animals roam freely, creating an authentic safari experience.

- **Big Mammals**: Giraffes, white rhinos, zebras, elands, buffaloes, and oryx.

- **Primates**: Patas monkeys and green monkeys are common sights.

- **Birdlife**: Over 120 species, including hornbills, eagles, and weaver birds.

- **Reptiles**: Observe Nile crocodiles basking near waterholes.

2. Baobab Forest

Bandia is home to majestic baobab trees, some over 1,000 years old. One of the most remarkable baobabs serves as a "cemetery tree," a resting place for the remains of the Serer people, reflecting local traditions.

What to Expect on Your Visit

1. Guided Safari Tours

Tours are conducted in open safari vehicles, allowing for unobstructed views of the landscape and wildlife. Guides share fascinating insights into the reserve's animals, their behaviors, and the ecological importance of the park.

- **Duration**: Approximately 2 hours.
- **Best Time to Visit**: Morning tours are ideal for cooler weather and more active animals.

2. Observation Decks and Rest Areas

The reserve has shaded observation platforms overlooking watering holes. These are perfect for watching wildlife gather and interact.

3. On-Site Facilities

- **Restaurant and Bar**: Located near the entrance, serving Senegalese and international cuisine. Try their grilled chicken or fresh fish dishes.
- **Souvenir Shop**: Features locally made crafts, wildlife-themed art, and apparel.

Nearby Attractions for Extended Excursions

1. Saly Portudal (20-minute drive)

- **Activities**: Beaches, water sports, and vibrant nightlife.

- **Dining**: Enjoy fresh seafood at La Riviera.
- **Accommodation**: The Lamantin Beach Resort & Spa offers luxury stays.

2. Mbour (25-minute drive)

- **Highlights**: Visit the fishing port to see colorful pirogues and bustling fish markets.
- **Dining**: Le Petit Zing serves traditional Senegalese dishes.

Planning Your Visit

Transportation Options

1. **Private Vehicles**: Renting a car is convenient for reaching the reserve. Make sure your rental includes a driver familiar with the area.
2. **Tours and Excursions**: Many operators in Dakar and Saly offer packages that include transport, entry fees, and guided tours.
3. **Taxis**: While more expensive, hiring a taxi for the day ensures flexibility and comfort.

What to Bring

- Comfortable clothing and sturdy footwear suitable for walking in dusty conditions.
- Sunscreen, sunglasses, and a hat for sun protection.
- Binoculars for birdwatching and a good camera for capturing memories.
- Drinking water, though refreshments are available at the restaurant.

Dining Recommendations Nearby

If you want to dine outside the reserve:

1. **La Guinguette, Saly**: Known for its seafood platters and serene garden setting.
2. **Le Petit Maroc, Mbour**: Offers Moroccan cuisine with a Senegalese twist.

Accommodations Near Bandia Wildlife Reserve

For visitors planning an overnight stay:

1. **Baobab Soleil Lodge**: A charming eco-lodge located just a few kilometers from the reserve. Offers rustic yet comfortable accommodations surrounded by nature.
2. **Royal Decameron Baobab, La Somone**: A luxury beachfront resort offering stunning views and all-inclusive services.
3. **Hôtel Keur Marrakis, Mbour**: A budget-friendly option with cozy rooms and easy access to both the reserve and nearby attractions.

Eco-Conservation Efforts

Bandia Wildlife Reserve plays a crucial role in preserving Senegal's biodiversity. Many of the species found here, such as white rhinos and giraffes, were reintroduced after disappearing from the region due to hunting and habitat loss. Visitors contribute to these efforts by supporting the park through entry fees and purchases.

Tips for an Enriching Experience

1. **Respect Wildlife**: Maintain a safe distance from animals and avoid loud noises.
2. **Follow Guide Instructions**: Guides ensure both visitor safety and minimal disturbance to wildlife.

3. **Learn the History**: Engage with your guide about the cultural significance of the reserve and its ancient baobabs.

Sine-Saloum Delta

1. Exploring the Natural Beauty of the Sine-Saloum Delta

A. Unique Ecosystem

The Sine-Saloum Delta covers over 190,000 hectares of mangroves, lagoons, and islands, creating a mosaic of habitats. Its saline waters and lush vegetation support a wide range of wildlife, including over 200 bird species, dolphins, and manatees.

B. Birdwatching Paradise

- The delta is a haven for ornithologists. Spot flamingos, pelicans, herons, and even rare African spoonbills during a guided birdwatching tour.
- **Best Time**: October to March when migratory birds flock to the region.

2. Activities to Enjoy in the Sine-Saloum Delta

A. Boat Tours

- **Pirogue Rides**: Glide through the mangroves in a traditional canoe. Guides often share fascinating insights into the region's ecology and history.
- **Sunset Cruises**: Evening boat tours offer spectacular views of the sun dipping below the horizon, casting golden reflections on the water.

B. Fishing Excursions

- Join local fishermen for a day of artisanal fishing. Techniques like net casting and line fishing are demonstrated, and visitors often get to cook their catch afterward.

C. Kayaking Adventures

- Paddle through narrow waterways surrounded by dense mangroves. This activity is perfect for those seeking solitude and a closer connection with nature.

D. Cultural Experiences

- Visit **Djiffer Village** to see traditional fishing practices and meet local communities.
- Explore **Mar Lodj**, an island renowned for its baobab-lined paths, serene ambiance, and a church featuring African-style architecture.

3. Immersing in Local Culture

A. Traditional Serer and Wolof Villages

- The delta is home to the Serer and Wolof communities. Guided tours often include stops in villages where you can learn about local crafts, music, and storytelling traditions.

B. Culinary Workshops

- Participate in cooking classes led by village women. Learn to prepare iconic dishes like *Yassa Poulet* and use fresh, locally-sourced ingredients.

C. Festivals and Celebrations

- Time your visit during regional festivals to witness vibrant dances, drum performances, and community feasts.

4. Eco-Tourism and Conservation Efforts

The Sine-Saloum Delta is a prime example of sustainable tourism. Local initiatives aim to preserve its unique biodiversity while supporting community livelihoods.

A. Responsible Travel Tips

- Avoid single-use plastics to protect the marine ecosystem.
- Support local guides and eco-lodges that invest in conservation.

B. Volunteer Opportunities

- Programs like mangrove reforestation projects welcome visitors to contribute. Planting trees not only benefits the environment but also creates meaningful connections with the local community.

---

5. Must-See Attractions Within the Delta

A. Palmarin Reserve

- **Special Features**: Baobab groves and salt flats teeming with flamingos.
- **Best Activity**: Guided walks or cycling tours.

B. Sangomar Point

- A sandbar that forms a natural divide between the ocean and the delta. It's a perfect spot for photography and birdwatching.

C. Mangrove Forests

- Explore dense mangrove channels teeming with crabs and fish. The mangroves play a crucial role in protecting the coastline and supporting local fisheries.

---

6. Practical Tips for Your Excursion

A. What to Pack

- **Comfortable Shoes**: For walking tours and village visits.
- **Bug Repellent**: Protect against mosquitoes, especially in the evening.

- **Sun Protection**: A wide-brimmed hat, sunglasses, and sunscreen are essential.

B. Best Time to Visit

- **Dry Season (November to May)**: Ideal for exploring without heavy rains.
- **Green Season (June to October)**: Offers lush landscapes and increased bird activity but comes with occasional rain.

C. Accessibility

- The delta is about a 3-hour drive from Dakar. Private transport or organized tours are recommended for hassle-free travel.

---

7. Dining Options in the Delta

- **Island Picnics**: Many boat tours include stops on secluded islands for picnics featuring fresh seafood.
- **Local Restaurants**: Enjoy authentic Senegalese meals prepared with freshly caught fish and local produce.

---

8. Accommodation Options for Longer Stays

A. Lodge Recommendations

- **Eco-Lodge du Sine-Saloum**: Offers eco-friendly bungalows with guided delta tours.
- **Les Palétuviers**: A luxurious retreat with stunning views and a spa.

B. Camping

For adventurous travelers, camping on the delta's islands provides a closer connection to nature. Local operators often arrange tented camps with meals included.

---

9. Memorable Experiences to Take Home

- Witness a fisherman's song echoing through the mangroves.
- Take home unique souvenirs like handwoven baskets or traditional shell necklaces crafted by local artisans.
- Capture breathtaking photos of flamingos silhouetted against the sunrise.

CHAPTER 12.

PRACTICAL INFORMATION

Managing your finances effectively is a crucial aspect of any trip, and Senegal offers a dynamic mix of cash-based and digital financial services. With the right preparation, you can navigate its monetary landscape smoothly, ensuring a seamless and enjoyable experience.

Currency and Money Matters

1. Currency Exchange Tips

A. Arrival Preparation

- Bring USD, EUR, or GBP in cash, as these are the most commonly accepted foreign currencies for exchange.
- Avoid exchanging money at the airport due to unfavorable rates.

B. Reliable Exchange Services

1. **Banks**:
   - Recommended for safety and transparency.
   - Major banks include:
     - *Ecobank Senegal*: Nationwide branches and 24/7 ATMs.
     - *BNP Paribas Senegal*: Offers competitive rates and English-speaking staff.
2. **Exchange Bureaus**:

- Known for convenience but ensure you verify rates and count your cash on-site.
- Example: *Bureau de Change ACSA* in Dakar.
- Address: 30 Avenue Blaise Diagne, Dakar.
- Opening Hours: Daily, 9:00 AM – 8:00 PM.

C. Pro Tips

- Avoid street vendors offering currency exchange; scams and counterfeit notes are risks.
- Request smaller denominations, as many vendors and taxis lack change for larger bills.

---

2. Using ATMs in Senegal

A. Availability

- ATMs are widely available in urban areas like Dakar, Saint-Louis, and Saly.
- Look for machines operated by reputable banks such as **Société Générale Senegal** or **Ecobank**.

B. Withdrawal Limits and Fees

- Withdrawal limits range between 50,000 and 200,000 F CFA per transaction.
- International transaction fees can vary depending on your home bank, typically between 2-5%.

C. Tips for ATM Use

- Opt for ATMs located inside bank premises for enhanced security.
- Notify your home bank about your travel plans to avoid flagged transactions.

---

3. Credit and Debit Card Usage

A. Acceptance

- Credit cards like **Visa** and **MasterCard** are widely accepted in urban areas, high-end restaurants, and hotels.
- In rural or smaller towns, cash remains the primary mode of payment.

B. Transaction Fees

- Foreign transaction fees range between 1-3% of the purchase amount.

C. Emergency Backup

- Always carry cash as a backup, especially for transport, local markets, or small eateries.

---

4. Mobile Payment Options

A. Mobile Wallets in Senegal

- Services like **Orange Money** and **Wari** are widely used for peer-to-peer transfers, utility payments, and even purchases at some stores.
- To use these, you'll need a local SIM card and registration with the service provider.

B. Benefits

- Instant transactions with minimal fees.
- Convenient for small purchases and payments.

---

5. Budgeting Your Trip

A. Typical Daily Costs

- **Accommodation**:

- o   Budget: 10,000 – 20,000 F CFA ($16 – $33 USD) per night for hostels or guesthouses.
- o   Mid-range: 30,000 – 60,000 F CFA ($50 – $100 USD) for boutique hotels.
- o   Luxury: 100,000 F CFA ($165 USD) and above.
- **Meals**:
  - o   Street food: 1,000 – 2,500 F CFA ($1.50 – $4 USD).
  - o   Mid-range restaurants: 5,000 – 10,000 F CFA ($8 – $16 USD) per meal.
  - o   Fine dining: 15,000 F CFA ($25 USD) and above.
- **Transport**:
  - o   Shared taxis: 1,000 F CFA ($1.50 USD) for short rides.
  - o   Intercity buses: 3,000 – 10,000 F CFA ($5 – $16 USD).

---

6. Tipping Culture in Senegal

A. Common Practices

- Tipping is appreciated but not mandatory.
- Restaurants: 5-10% of the bill.
- Guides and drivers: 2,000 – 5,000 F CFA ($3 – $8 USD) depending on service quality.

B. Pro Tips

- Always tip in local currency.
- For exceptional service, a higher tip is welcomed.

---

7. Security and Safety for Money Matters

A. Counterfeit Risks

- Familiarize yourself with the look and feel of genuine CFA Franc notes.
- Avoid accepting torn or damaged bills, as they may not be accepted by vendors.

B. Theft Prevention

- Use money belts or concealed pouches to store your cash securely.
- Avoid carrying large amounts of cash, especially in crowded areas.

C. Emergency Assistance

- Contact your embassy if you lose access to funds. Most embassies can facilitate emergency cash transfers.

---

8. Recommendations for Travelers

A. Best Practices for Currency Exchange

- Exchange a small amount of cash before arriving in Senegal to cover immediate expenses like taxis.
- Keep a mix of denominations for flexibility during transactions.

B. Navigating Remote Areas

- In rural regions, ATMs are scarce, and cash is king. Plan accordingly by withdrawing enough money before leaving urban areas.

C. Digital Payment Trends

- As mobile payment adoption continues to grow, consider using local wallets like Orange Money for convenient, cashless transactions.

Mobile Connectivity and Internet Access

1. Setting Up Mobile Connectivity in Senegal

A. Purchasing a SIM Card

Getting a local SIM card is straightforward and essential for cost-effective communication.

- **Where to Buy**:
    - Airports: Shops are available at Blaise Diagne International Airport.
    - Official Stores: Visit Orange, Free, or Expresso outlets in cities like Dakar and Thiès.
    - Street Vendors: Common but avoid unregistered SIM cards to prevent issues.

B. Registration Process

- **Requirements**: Passport or a valid form of ID.
- **Process**: Registration takes about 10-15 minutes at authorized outlets. Your SIM card is usually activated instantly.

C. Compatibility

- Ensure your phone is unlocked and supports GSM networks (common in most modern smartphones).

---

2. Data Plans and Coverage

A. Popular Plans by Provider

1. **Orange Senegal**:
    - Daily plans (500 CFA for 1 GB).
    - Monthly plans (10,000 CFA for 50 GB).

2. **Free Senegal**:
    - Daily (300 CFA for 500 MB).
    - Monthly (5,000 CFA for 20 GB).
3. **Expresso Senegal**:
    - Daily (200 CFA for 200 MB).
    - Monthly (7,500 CFA for unlimited access with fair usage policy).

B. Coverage Quality

- **Urban Areas**: Excellent 4G coverage in cities like Dakar, Saint-Louis, and Ziguinchor.
- **Rural Areas**: Coverage can be inconsistent; 3G or 2G networks are more common in remote areas.

---

3. Mobile Internet for Travelers

A. Pocket Wi-Fi Devices

- **Rental Providers**: Available at the airport or through companies like WiSenegal.
- **Cost**: Around 5,000 CFA ($8.50 USD) per day, including 10 GB of data.

B. Tethering and Hotspots

- Using your smartphone as a hotspot is a convenient option if your data plan supports it.

---

4. Internet Access in Remote Areas

A. Satellite Internet

- Ideal for extended stays in regions like Casamance or the Sine-Saloum Delta.

- Providers such as HughesNet and local companies offer packages starting at 20,000 CFA ($34 USD) per month.

B. Community Centers

- Many villages have community telecenters equipped with basic internet access.

---

5. Free and Paid Wi-Fi Options

A. Airports and Transportation Hubs

- Blaise Diagne International Airport offers free Wi-Fi for up to two hours.

B. Hotels and Resorts

- Luxury hotels like *Terrou-Bi* in Dakar provide high-speed internet.

C. Public Spaces

- Wi-Fi hotspots in city parks and plazas, often free but requiring registration.

---

6. Cybersecurity and Safe Browsing

A. Using Public Wi-Fi

- Avoid accessing sensitive information (e.g., online banking) over unsecured networks.
- Use VPNs for added security; providers like NordVPN or ExpressVPN have strong connections in Senegal.

B. Protecting Mobile Devices

- Install antivirus software to prevent malware.
- Keep your phone and apps updated for optimal security.

---

7. Tips for Staying Connected While Traveling

A. Optimize Data Usage

- Use data-saving modes on apps like YouTube or Google Maps.
- Download maps and guides offline when planning trips to areas with limited connectivity.

B. Communication Apps

- **WhatsApp**: Widely used in Senegal for messaging and calls.
- **Skype or Zoom**: For video calls, especially when using high-speed Wi-Fi.

C. Emergency Numbers

- Store essential contacts, including embassy and local emergency services, for quick access.

---

8. Dining and Accommodation with Connectivity

A. Restaurants

- *La Calebasse* in Dakar: Free Wi-Fi alongside its traditional Senegalese menu.
- *Ziguinchor Café*: A hub for travelers in Casamance with reliable internet.

B. Hotels

- Budget: *Hotel Baraka* in Dakar offers basic but reliable internet.
- Luxury: *Radisson Blu Dakar Sea Plaza* provides high-speed Wi-Fi in all rooms and common areas.

---

9. Troubleshooting and Customer Support

A. Common Issues

1. **SIM Activation Delays**: Contact the provider's customer service directly.

2. **Poor Coverage in Rural Areas**: Consider upgrading to a satellite plan.

B. Customer Support Numbers

- Orange Senegal: 1441
- Free Senegal: 1234
- Expresso Senegal: 1212

---

10. Planning Your Connectivity for Excursions

A. Remote Areas

- Download maps and travel apps for offline use before heading to places like Niokolo-Koba National Park.

B. Group Travel

- Sharing a pocket Wi-Fi device can reduce individual data costs.

13.3. Emergency Numbers and Contacts

Healthcare Facilities and Medical Contacts

A. Hospitals and Clinics in Major Cities

1. **Principal Hospital of Dakar (Hôpital Principal de Dakar)**

   - **Address**: Avenue Nelson Mandela, Dakar.
   - **Opening Times**: 24/7 for emergencies.
   - **Contact**: +221 33 839 50 50.
   - **Pricing**: Consultation fees typically start from 15,000 CFA ($25 USD).

- o **Specialization**: Equipped for critical care, surgery, and specialized treatments.

2. **Fann University Hospital (Centre Hospitalier Universitaire de Fann)**
   - o **Address**: Route de Ouakam, Dakar.
   - o **Opening Times**: 24/7 for emergencies; outpatient services 8:00 AM – 5:00 PM.
   - o **Contact**: +221 33 839 75 00.
   - o **Pricing**: Consultation fees vary based on specialty.
   - o **Specialization**: Infectious diseases, neurology, and psychiatry.

3. **Regional Hospital of Saint-Louis**
   - o **Address**: Avenue Blaise Diagne, Saint-Louis.
   - o **Opening Times**: 24/7 for emergencies.
   - o **Contact**: +221 33 961 24 24.
   - o **Specialization**: General healthcare and obstetrics.

4. **Clinique Madeleine**
   - o **Address**: Rue Carnot, Dakar Plateau.
   - o **Opening Times**: 24/7.
   - o **Contact**: +221 33 889 25 25.
   - o **Pricing**: Higher-end private clinic; consultations start around 25,000 CFA ($42 USD).
   - o **Specialization**: Private healthcare with English-speaking staff.

B. Pharmacies

Pharmacies in Senegal are well-stocked with both prescription and over-the-counter medicines.

- **Hours**: Most are open from 8:00 AM to 9:00 PM.
- **Emergency Pharmacy Services**: A rotating schedule ensures one pharmacy per area is open 24/7.

Key Emergency Pharmacy:

- **Dakar Plateau**: Pharmacie Kër Cheikh, Avenue Lamine Guèye, Dakar.

Embassies and Consulates

Tourists should note the contact information for their country's embassy or consulate in Dakar for assistance with legal, medical, or emergency matters.

Major Embassies in Dakar

1. **United States Embassy**
   - **Address**: Route des Almadies, Dakar.
   - **Opening Times**: Monday–Thursday, 8:00 AM – 5:00 PM; Friday, 8:00 AM – 1:00 PM.
   - **Contact**: +221 33 879 40 00.
2. **French Embassy**
   - **Address**: 1 Rue El Hadji Amadou Assane Ndoye, Dakar.
   - **Opening Times**: Monday–Friday, 8:30 AM – 12:30 PM.
   - **Contact**: +221 33 839 52 00.
3. **British Embassy**
   - **Address**: Rue des Almadies, Dakar.
   - **Opening Times**: Monday–Thursday, 8:30 AM – 4:30 PM; Friday, 8:30 AM – 1:00 PM.
   - **Contact**: +221 33 823 73 92.

Key Contacts for Non-Emergency Assistance

1. **Tourism Bureau of Senegal**

    o   **Contact**: +221 33 823 64 99.

    o   **Purpose**: Provides travel information, maps, and safety guidelines.

2. **Air Travel and Lost Baggage**

    o   **Blaise Diagne International Airport (DSS)**

        ▪   **Contact**: +221 33 959 69 69 (General Inquiries).

        ▪   **Lost and Found**: +221 33 959 70 10.

3. **Local Transportation Helpline**

    o   **Contact**: +221 33 889 04 00 (for inquiries on public transport or taxis).

Safety Tips for Emergencies

A. Carry Essential Information

- Write down or save in your phone the key emergency numbers and embassy contacts.

- Have a copy of your travel insurance details readily available.

B. Understanding Local Protocols

- Police and emergency responders are usually French-speaking. If you do not speak French, consider having basic phrases or a translator app on hand.

C. Emergency Preparedness Kit

- Keep a small first-aid kit, a power bank, and a flashlight for emergencies.

D. Insurance Coverage

- Ensure your travel insurance includes medical evacuation coverage, as advanced treatments might require transfer to another country.

Dining and Accommodation Recommendations for Nearby Assistance

Dakar

- **Dining**:
    - *Le Relais de l'Espadon*: Near the U.S. Embassy, offering international cuisine.
    - *La Fourchette*: A high-end option for French and Senegalese dishes.
- **Accommodation**:
    - *Radisson Blu Hotel Dakar Sea Plaza*: Centrally located with emergency contact services.

Saint-Louis

- **Dining**:
    - *La Linguère*: Offers a cozy ambiance and fresh seafood.
- **Accommodation**:
    - *Hotel Mermoz*: Popular among tourists, with a 24-hour reception desk for assistance.

CHAPTER 13.

SUGGESTED ITINERARIES

Senegal offers a vibrant tapestry of culture, history, and natural beauty that can be explored in a well-planned one-week itinerary. This guide provides a comprehensive day-by-day breakdown of the best experiences to maximize your time in Senegal. Whether you're a cultural enthusiast, nature lover, or history buff, this itinerary offers a seamless and enriching travel experience.

One-Week Highlights of Senegal

Day 1: Arrival in Dakar and Exploring the City

Morning: Arrival and Check-In

- **Accommodation Suggestion**:
- **Radisson Blu Hotel, Dakar Sea Plaza**
  - Address: Route de la Corniche Ouest, Dakar.
  - Price: From $200 USD/night.
  - Amenities: Sea-facing rooms, infinity pool, and close proximity to major attractions.

Afternoon: Gorée Island

- **Gorée Island (Île de Gorée)**: A UNESCO World Heritage site.
  - **Ferry Terminal**: Gare Maritime de Dakar.
  - **Opening Hours**: 8:00 AM–6:00 PM.

- - **Pricing**: Ferry round-trip (~5,200 CFA, $9 USD). Gorée entry fee ~500 CFA ($1 USD).
- Explore:
  - **Maison des Esclaves (House of Slaves)**: Emotional history of the transatlantic slave trade.
  - Quaint colonial streets and artisan markets.

Evening: Local Cuisine

- **Dinner Recommendation**:
- **Chez Loutcha** (Rue Carnot, Dakar).
  - Signature Dishes: Thieboudienne (Senegalese jollof) and Yassa Poulet.
  - Price: ~$10–$20 USD per meal.

Day 2: Lac Rose (Pink Lake)

Morning: Departure to Lac Rose

- **Distance**: ~1 hour from Dakar.
- **Transport Option**: Private taxi (~15,000 CFA, $25 USD).
- **Entry Fee**: ~2,000 CFA ($3 USD).

Activities:

- Witness the lake's pink hue caused by high salt content and microorganisms.
- **Salt Harvesting Tours**: Join locals collecting salt—immersive and educational.
- Camel rides or quad biking around the lake.

Lunch:

- **Restaurant Chez Salim**
  - Price: ~5,000 CFA ($8 USD).
  - Must-Try: Grilled fish with fresh vegetables.

Evening: **Return to Dakar for rest.**

Day 3: Bandia Wildlife Reserve

Morning: Safari Adventure

- **Address**: Bandia Reserve, ~65 km southeast of Dakar.
- **Opening Hours**: 9:00 AM–6:00 PM.
- **Entry Fee**: 12,000 CFA ($20 USD) per person.
- **Activities**:
  - Open-air safari tours to see giraffes, rhinos, zebras, and antelopes.
  - Guided tours available (~15,000 CFA for groups).

Lunch:

- **On-Site Restaurant**: Scenic views and traditional meals.

Afternoon: **Visit Joal-Fadiouth**

- **Distance**: ~1 hour from Bandia.
- **Key Highlights**:
  - The shell island of Fadiouth.
  - Mixed-faith cemetery with Christian and Muslim graves.
- **Entry Fee**: 2,500 CFA ($4 USD) for a guided tour.

Day 4: Saint-Louis – Colonial Charm

Morning: Drive to Saint-Louis

- **Distance**: ~4.5 hours from Dakar.
- **Transport**: Shared taxis (~6,000 CFA per person) or private car hire (~50,000 CFA).

Afternoon: **Exploring the City**

- **Must-Visit**:

- o **Faidherbe Bridge**: Iconic iron structure designed by Gustave Eiffel.
- o **Historic Quarter**: Quaint streets with colonial-era architecture.
- **Lunch Recommendation**:
- **La Résidence**: French-Senegalese fusion cuisine (~$20 USD per meal).

Evening: **Live Music**

- **Venue**: Ndar Ndar Music Festival (seasonal).

Day 5: Djoudj National Bird Sanctuary

Morning: Departure for Djoudj

- **Address**: ~60 km from Saint-Louis.
- **Opening Hours**: 7:00 AM–5:00 PM.
- **Entry Fee**: 10,000 CFA ($16 USD).

Activities:

- Boat tours to see over 400 species of migratory birds, including pelicans and flamingos.

Lunch: **Return to Saint-Louis for local seafood at** Flamingo Restaurant **(~$15 USD).**

Evening: **Sunset along the Langue de Barbarie.**

Day 6: Sine-Saloum Delta – Nature's Paradise

Morning: Drive to Sine-Saloum

- **Distance**: ~3 hours from Saint-Louis.

Accommodation Suggestion:

Ecolodge de Palmarin

- Price: ~40,000 CFA/night ($65 USD).
- Features: Sustainable lodges with mangrove views.

Activities:

- Guided canoe trips through mangroves.
- Visit traditional Serer fishing villages.
- Birdwatching and spotting manatees.

Lunch: **Freshly caught fish prepared locally (~$10 USD).**

Day 7: Return to Dakar and Relax

Morning: Return to Dakar

- Take your time and enjoy scenic stops along the way.

Afternoon: Souvenir Shopping

- **Location**: Sandaga Market.
  - Items: Beaded necklaces, fabric, and wooden carvings.
  - Tips: Bargain with confidence—start at half the quoted price.

Evening: Farewell Dinner

- **Restaurant Recommendation**:
- **Le Ngor Restaurant (Route de la Corniche)**
  - Sea-view dining with fresh seafood and modern Senegalese cuisine.
  - Price: ~$25 USD per meal.

Two-Week Adventure Across the Country

Day 1-2: Dakar - The Capital of West African Vibes

What to Do

1. **Gorée Island**

- Address: Ferry from Dakar Port, Boulevard de la Libération, Dakar.
- Opening Times: Daily, 7:00 AM–7:00 PM.
- Pricing: Round-trip ferry 5,200 CFA (~$8.50 USD) for tourists.
- Visit the House of Slaves (*Maison des Esclaves*), a poignant reminder of the transatlantic slave trade.
- Wander through cobblestone streets lined with colorful colonial houses.

2. **African Renaissance Monument**
   - Address: Route de Ouakam, Dakar.
   - Opening Times: Daily, 9:00 AM–6:00 PM.
   - Pricing: Entrance fee 6,000 CFA (~$10 USD).
   - Climb the monument for panoramic views of Dakar.

Dining Options

- **Le Lagon 1**: Seafood by the ocean, with dishes like grilled prawns (~15,000 CFA/$25 USD).
- **Chez Loutcha**: Traditional Senegalese cuisine like *thieboudienne* (rice and fish) (~5,000 CFA/$8 USD).

Accommodation

- **Terrou-Bi Hotel**: Luxury beachfront resort (~$200 USD/night).
- **Hotel Djoloff**: Boutique hotel with Senegalese décor (~$90 USD/night).

Day 3-4: Saint-Louis - Colonial Charm and Culture

What to Do

1. **Explore the Island of Saint-Louis**

- Address: Connected via Faidherbe Bridge from mainland.
- Opening Times: Open 24/7 for exploration.
- Walk through historic streets adorned with pastel-colored colonial buildings.

2. **Langue de Barbarie National Park**
   - **Address**: 20 km south of Saint-Louis.
   - **Opening Times**: Daily, 8:00 AM–5:00 PM.
   - **Pricing**: Park entrance fee 3,000 CFA (~$5 USD).
   - Enjoy birdwatching and boat tours along the Senegal River.

Dining Options

- **La Kora Chez Peggy**: Creole and Senegalese fusion, meals start at ~6,000 CFA ($10 USD).
- **Flamingo**: Riverside dining with fresh fish and salads (~7,000 CFA/$12 USD).

Accommodation

- **La Résidence**: Colonial-style boutique hotel (~$80 USD/night).
- **Hotel Cap Saint-Louis**: Mid-range option near the beach (~$50 USD/night).

Day 5-6: Sine-Saloum Delta - Nature and Tranquility

What to Do

1. **Delta Exploration by Pirogue**
   - **Address**: Departures from Ndangane or Toubacouta.
   - **Opening Times**: Tours start early, 7:00 AM–4:00 PM.
   - **Pricing**: Boat tour 10,000 CFA (~$16 USD).

- Marvel at mangroves, birdlife, and small fishing villages.

2. **Fathala Wildlife Reserve**
   - **Address**: Toubacouta, Sine-Saloum Delta.
   - **Opening Times**: Daily, 7:00 AM–6:00 PM.
   - **Pricing**: Safari tours 15,000 CFA (~$25 USD).
   - Spot giraffes, zebras, and rhinoceroses on a guided tour.

Dining Options

- **Keur Youssou**: Local seafood dishes like *yassa poisson* (~5,500 CFA/$9 USD).
- **Hotel Les Palétuviers**: Riverside dining with international options (~7,000 CFA/$12 USD).

Accommodation

- **Les Palétuviers**: Luxurious eco-lodge (~$120 USD/night).
- **Ecolodge de Simal**: Budget-friendly option (~$40 USD/night).

Day 7-8: Tambacounda and Niokolo-Koba National Park

What to Do

1. **Niokolo-Koba National Park Safari**
   - **Address**: Located 80 km southeast of Tambacounda.
   - **Opening Times**: Daily, 6:00 AM–6:00 PM.
   - **Pricing**: Park entrance fee 7,000 CFA (~$12 USD).
   - Witness lions, elephants, and hippos in their natural habitats.

2. **Hiking and Cultural Tours**
   - Trek through the park's trails and visit nearby villages to learn about local traditions.

Dining Options

- **Relais de Tambacounda**: Traditional and continental dishes (~6,000 CFA/$10 USD).
- **Campement Wassadou**: Simple yet hearty meals (~4,500 CFA/$7 USD).

Accommodation

- **Relais de Niokolo**: Comfortable lodges (~$50 USD/night).
- **Campement Wassadou**: Budget eco-lodges (~$35 USD/night).

Day 9-10: Casamance - Senegal's Green Paradise

What to Do

1. **Ziguinchor City Tour**

   o Explore vibrant markets and colonial architecture.

2. **Cap Skirring Beaches**

   o **Address**: Cap Skirring, Casamance Region.

   o **Opening Times**: Open all day.

   o Relax on white-sand beaches or enjoy water sports like kayaking and windsurfing.

Dining Options

- **La Paillote**: Fine dining with seafood platters (~12,000 CFA/$20 USD).
- **Chez Sadio**: Casual, family-style meals (~5,000 CFA/$8 USD).

Accommodation

- **Le Cap Ocean**: Luxury beachfront resort (~$150 USD/night).
- **Motel le Kadiandoumagne**: Mid-range, riverside rooms (~$60 USD/night).

Day 11-12: Lac Rose and Bandia Reserve

What to Do

1. **Lac Rose (Pink Lake)**

   o **Address**: 30 km from Dakar, Niaga Village.

   o **Opening Times**: Daily, 8:00 AM–6:00 PM.

   o **Pricing**: Entry and guided tours ~~5,000 CFA~~ ($8 USD).

   o Witness the lake's vibrant pink hues and learn about salt harvesting.

2. **Bandia Reserve Safari**

   o **Address**: 65 km from Dakar.

   o **Opening Times**: Daily, 8:00 AM–6:00 PM.

   o **Pricing**: Safari fee 15,000 CFA (~$25 USD).

   o Spot giraffes, buffaloes, and antelopes.

Dining Options

- **Chez Salim**: Local dishes at Lac Rose (~6,000 CFA/$10 USD).

- **Bandia Lodge Restaurant**: Traditional meals post-safari (~7,500 CFA/$12 USD).

Accommodation

- **Chez Salim**: Comfortable lakeside rooms (~$50 USD/night).

- **Bandia Lodge**: Rustic safari-style accommodations (~$80 USD/night).

Day 13-14: Return to Dakar and Wrap Up

What to Do

- Shop for souvenirs at Sandaga Market.

- Enjoy a farewell dinner at **Ngor Island**, a short pirogue ride from Dakar.

Dining Options

- **Ngor Lounge**: Fusion dishes with ocean views (~12,000 CFA/$20 USD).
- **La Galette**: Casual bistro (~7,000 CFA/$12 USD).

Accommodation

- **Radisson Blu Hotel Dakar Sea Plaza**: Luxury retreat (~$200 USD/night).
- **Yaas Hotel Almadies**: Budget-friendly with modern amenities (~$60 USD/night).

Special Interest Itineraries (Cultural, Wildlife, or Relaxation-Focused)

1. Cultural Exploration Itinerary (7 Days)

Day 1: Dakar – The Vibrant Capital

- **Morning**: Visit the **IFAN Museum of African Arts** (Address: Place de Soweto, Dakar).
  - Opening Hours: Tue-Sun, 9:00 AM–6:00 PM.
  - Entry Fee: 2,000 CFA ($3 USD).
  - Highlights: Traditional African artifacts, textiles, and carvings.
- **Afternoon**: Take a ferry to **Gorée Island**.
  - Ferry Terminal: Port de Dakar.
  - Ferry Timings: Hourly from 7:00 AM to 11:00 PM.
  - Fee: 5,200 CFA ($8 USD round trip).
  - Key Spot: House of Slaves (Maison des Esclaves).
- **Evening**: Dinner at **Chez Loutcha** (Address: 101 Rue Moussé Diop, Dakar).

- o Cuisine: Authentic Senegalese dishes like *thiéboudienne*.
- o Cost: ~10,000 CFA ($16 USD).

Day 2: Saint-Louis – Colonial Charm

- **Morning**: Drive to Saint-Louis (4.5 hours from Dakar). Stay at **La Résidence Saint-Louis** (Price: $50–$80 USD/night).
- **Afternoon**: Explore the **Historical Quarter**.
    - o Highlights: Colonial-era architecture and colorful fishing boats at the quay.
- **Evening**: Enjoy jazz music at the **Saint-Louis Jazz Club**.

Day 3: Linguère – Fula Culture

- **Morning**: Visit a traditional Fula village near Linguère.
    - o Activity: Participate in a cultural workshop on music and dance.
    - o Cost: 15,000 CFA ($25 USD).

Day 4-5: Sine-Saloum Delta

- **Stay**: **Ecolodge de Palmarin** (Cost: $120 USD/night).
- Activities:
    - o Day 4: Traditional wrestling match (*Laamb*).
    - o Day 5: Fishing with local communities.

Day 6-7: Casamance

- **Highlights**: Explore Diola culture, sacred forests, and music performances.

2. Wildlife Adventure Itinerary (5 Days)

Day 1: Bandia Wildlife Reserve

- **Morning**: Safari at **Bandia Reserve** (Address: 65 km from Dakar, near Saly).
    - o Opening Hours: Daily, 7:00 AM–5:00 PM.
    - o Entry Fee: 12,000 CFA ($20 USD).

o Highlights: Giraffes, rhinos, zebras.

- **Afternoon**: Lunch at the reserve's restaurant overlooking a waterhole.

Day 2-3: Djoudj National Bird Sanctuary

- **Stay**: **Campement du Djoudj** (Cost: $40 USD/night).
- Activities:
  o Morning boat tours to view pelicans and flamingos.
  o Bird photography sessions.

Day 4: Fathala Wildlife Reserve

- **Morning**: Lion walk experience.
  o Cost: 25,000 CFA ($40 USD).

Day 5: Saloum Delta

- Kayaking through mangroves to spot aquatic birds.

3. Relaxation and Wellness Itinerary (5 Days)

Day 1: Somone Lagoon

- **Stay**: **Royal Horizon Baobab** (Cost: $150 USD/night).
- Activities: Yoga on the beach and sunset boat cruises.

Day 2-3: Cap Skirring

- **Stay**: **Les Alizes Beach Resort**.
- Activities: Spa treatments, beachfront lounging, and private cabana dining.

Day 4: Ngor Island

- Tranquil beaches and fresh seafood dinners.

Day 5: Lac Rose

- Therapeutic mud baths and salt harvesting tours.

CONCLUSION

As your journey to Senegal draws near, preparation is key to ensuring an unforgettable experience in this culturally vibrant and geographically diverse West African nation.

Final Travel Reminders

Important Addresses, Opening Times, and Costs

Visa and Entry Requirements

- **Address for Visa Services (if required)**: Senegalese Embassy or Consulate in your country.
- **Opening Times**: Typically 9:00 AM to 4:00 PM, Monday to Friday (varies by location).
- **Costs**: Tourist visas range from $50–$100, depending on duration. Ensure your passport is valid for at least six months beyond your travel dates.

Emergency Contact Numbers

- **General Emergency (Police)**: 17.
- **Medical Emergency**: 15.
- **Fire Services**: 18.
- **Tourist Assistance**: Ministry of Tourism Dakar Office: +221 33 889 8920.

Transportation Hubs

- **Dakar Blaise Diagne International Airport (DSS)**
    - **Opening Hours**: 24/7.

- o **Services**: Currency exchange, SIM cards, and taxis readily available.
- o **Pricing**: Taxi to Dakar city center ~15,000 CFA ($25 USD).
- **Bus and Minivan Terminals**: Gare Routière de Pompiers (Dakar).
  - o **Opening Times**: 6:00 AM–8:00 PM.
  - o **Pricing**: Intercity fares start from 5,000 CFA ($8 USD).

Health and Safety Tips

1. **Vaccinations**: Yellow fever vaccination is mandatory; bring your certificate.
2. **Medical Facilities**:
   - o **Address for Clinics in Dakar**: Clinique de la Madeleine, Avenue Nelson Mandela.
   - o **Opening Times**: 24/7 emergency services.
   - o **Cost**: Consultation fees start at 10,000 CFA ($16 USD).
3. **Travel Insurance**: Comprehensive travel insurance is strongly recommended to cover medical expenses and emergencies.

Currency and Spending

- **Currency**: West African CFA Franc (XOF).
- **Conversion Rate**: 1 USD ≈ 600 CFA (subject to fluctuation).
- **Tips**:
  - o ATMs are widely available in urban areas but may not accept all card types.
  - o Carry small denominations for local markets or tipping.

Packing and Essentials

1. Weather-Appropriate Clothing

Senegal's climate varies by region and season:

- **Dry Season (November to May)**: Lightweight cotton clothing, hats, and sunglasses for sunny days.
- **Rainy Season (June to October)**: Waterproof jackets and quick-drying footwear.

2. Photography Gear

- **Must-Have Items**:
  - DSLR or mirrorless camera for landscapes and wildlife.
  - A sturdy tripod for capturing low-light scenes or night skies.
  - Power bank for charging devices during day trips.

3. Local Adaptations

- **Electrical Outlets**: Senegal uses Type C and E plugs; voltage is 230V.
- **SIM Cards**: Purchase SIM cards from Orange or Free Mobile at airports or kiosks for connectivity.
- **Language Guide**: Learning basic Wolof or French phrases can enhance your interactions.

Dining and Accommodation Reminders

Top Dining Options

1. **Chez Loutcha (Dakar)**
   - **Cuisine**: Traditional Senegalese dishes.
   - **Address**: Avenue Hassan II, Dakar.
   - **Opening Hours**: 11:00 AM–10:00 PM.
   - **Pricing**: Main courses start at 4,000 CFA ($7 USD).

2. **Café des Arts (Saint-Louis)**

   o **Cuisine**: Fusion of local and international.

   o **Photographic Appeal**: Colonial architecture with a chic vibe.

Accommodation Highlights

1. **Radisson Blu (Dakar)**

   o **Address**: Route de la Corniche Ouest, Dakar.

   o **Price Range**: From $180 per night.

   o **Amenities**: Ocean views, infinity pools, and fine dining.

2. **Lodge des Collines de Niassam (Sine-Saloum Delta)**

   o **Specialty**: Treehouse and waterfront stays.

   o **Pricing**: ~45,000 CFA ($75 USD) per night.

Cultural Etiquette and Behavior

1. **Respect Local Customs**:

   o When visiting religious sites, dress modestly and remove shoes.

   o Greet with a handshake or a polite "As-salamu alaykum."

2. **Photography Consent**:

   o Always ask for permission before photographing people or cultural ceremonies.

Sustainability Tips

1. **Minimize Plastic Use**: Carry reusable water bottles.

2. **Support Local Artisans**: Purchase handmade crafts at markets like Sandaga or Soumbedioune.

3. **Responsible Wildlife Tourism**: Avoid attractions that exploit animals.

Sample Itinerary for Final Days

Day 1: Exploring Dakar

- Morning: Visit the African Renaissance Monument for panoramic views.
- Afternoon: Explore the Village des Arts, home to local artists.
- Evening: Sunset at Corniche Ouest followed by dinner at La Fourchette.

Day 2: Historical Journey

- Morning: Ferry to Gorée Island for a historical tour.
- Afternoon: Relax at Gorée's beachside cafes.
- Evening: Return to Dakar; enjoy live music at Just 4 U jazz club.

Day 3: Natural Wonders

- Full day: Excursion to the Bandia Wildlife Reserve or Sine-Saloum Delta.

16.2. Inspiring Quotes about Senegal

1. "Teranga is more than hospitality; it is a philosophy of life."

- **Explanation**: Teranga, Senegal's defining cultural ethos, goes beyond simply welcoming guests. It embodies generosity, warmth, and community—a true reflection of the Senegalese spirit.
- **Connection to Your Journey**: Visitors often feel embraced as family, whether in bustling cities like Dakar or serene villages in the Casamance.

2. "The baobab tree is not just a tree; it is a monument of resilience and wisdom."

- **Visual Appeal**: Senegal's iconic baobab trees, scattered across its landscapes, are a symbol of endurance.

- **Suggested Activities**:
  - Visit the Sacred Baobab of Bandia, a tree hollowed by time yet revered by locals.
  - Capture its unique silhouette against the fiery hues of a Senegalese sunset.
  - **Address**: Bandia Reserve, near Saly; open daily 7:00 AM–5:00 PM; entry fee ~12,000 CFA ($20 USD).

3. "Senegal's music speaks to the soul of the world." **– Youssou N'Dour**

- **Meaning**: As a celebrated Senegalese musician, N'Dour encapsulates the global reach of the country's rhythms, from traditional sabar drumming to Afrobeat-infused mbalax.
- **Activity**: Attend live music performances at venues like Just 4 U in Dakar.
  - **Address**: Rue Carnot, Dakar.
  - **Timing**: Open daily 6:00 PM–midnight.
  - **Pricing**: Entry tickets vary (~3,000–7,000 CFA).

Historical Perspectives Rooted in Senegal

4. "Gorée Island is not just a place; it is a testimony to humanity's resilience."

- **Significance**: The House of Slaves (*Maison des Esclaves*) on Gorée Island serves as a somber reminder of the transatlantic slave trade, yet also as a tribute to survival and hope.
- **Visit Details**:
  - **Address**: Ferry terminal at Port de Dakar to Gorée Island.
  - **Timing**: Open daily 8:00 AM–6:00 PM.
  - **Pricing**: Museum entry ~500 CFA ($1 USD); ferry ~5,200 CFA ($8 USD).

- **Photography Tip**: Focus on the Door of No Return with its stark framing of the Atlantic Ocean.

5. "Saint-Louis is where time slows down, and history breathes through every brick."

- **Relevance**: As Senegal's first French settlement, Saint-Louis is a UNESCO World Heritage Site known for its colonial charm.
- **Highlights**: The Faidherbe Bridge, colorful colonial facades, and horse-drawn carriages.
    - **Address**: Saint-Louis, Northern Senegal.
    - **Pricing**: Guided tours ~8,000 CFA ($13 USD).
- **Dining Suggestion**: Relais de l'Espadon on the waterfront offers local seafood delights in a picturesque setting.

Quotes Reflecting Nature's Majesty

6. "The Pink Lake mirrors the joy of life in its rosy embrace."

- **Why It Matters**: Lac Rose (Pink Lake) is a natural wonder that changes hues with the seasons, symbolizing adaptability and beauty.
- **Experience**:
    - Boat rides to explore the lake and salt harvesting.
    - **Address**: Niaga, ~30 km from Dakar.
    - **Timing**: Open sunrise to sunset; guided tours ~10,000 CFA ($16 USD).

7. "The Senegal River flows with the stories of an ancient land."

- **Insight**: A lifeline for the north, the Senegal River supports agriculture, fishing, and transport while offering a tranquil setting for exploration.
- **Excursion Idea**: Take a traditional pirogue ride near Podor or Richard-Toll.

Modern Voices on Senegal's Future

8. "Senegal is a rising star, where tradition meets innovation."

- **Interpretation**: Senegal's progress, marked by initiatives like the African Renaissance Monument, highlights its blend of heritage and modernity.
  - **Visit Details**:
    - **Address**: Ouakam district, Dakar.
    - **Timing**: Open daily 9:00 AM–5:00 PM.
    - **Pricing**: Entry ~3,000 CFA ($5 USD).
  - **Best View**: Capture the monument from below to emphasize its towering presence.

Personal Reflections for Your Journey

9. "Traveling in Senegal, you'll find that the soul of the place is in its people."

- **Takeaway**: Beyond the landscapes and monuments, Senegal's true treasure lies in its vibrant communities.

10. "Teranga is not just a word; it's the feeling you take home."

- **Encouragement**: As you leave Senegal, carry the spirit of Teranga—its warmth, kindness, and open-heartedness—with you.

Recommended Final Stops

Before concluding your Senegal adventure, consider visiting:

- **The Sandaga Market** for last-minute souvenirs.
- **The Dakar Corniche** for one last view of the Atlantic Ocean.
- **Restaurant Le Lagon**:
  - **Address**: Route de la Corniche Est, Dakar.
  - **Timing**: Open 12:00 PM–11:00 PM.

      ○   **Specialties**: Seafood platters and panoramic views of the ocean.

16.3. How to Share Your Travel Stories

1. Curating Your Travel Content

Organize Your Notes and Photos

Before sharing, compile all your materials:

- **Photos**: Organize by location or theme, e.g., "Saint-Louis Jazz Festival," "Lac Rose Reflections," or "Sine-Saloum Delta Wildlife."
- **Journal Entries**: Highlight memorable experiences, funny anecdotes, and interactions with locals.

Tip: Use tools like Google Photos or Adobe Lightroom to sort and edit your images.

Structure Your Story

Break down your narrative into digestible sections:

1. **Introduction**: Set the scene with an overview of Senegal's unique charm.
2. **Main Body**: Share detailed experiences of places, food, and activities.
3. **Conclusion**: Reflect on what the trip meant to you and what others can take away from it.

Example:

For a day at Gorée Island:

- Morning: Describe the ferry ride and first impressions.
- Afternoon: Detail the visit to the *House of Slaves* and its emotional impact.
- Evening: Capture the sunset views and your thoughts as you left the island.

Select a Narrative Angle

Choose a unique perspective to tell your story.

- **Cultural Enthusiast**: Focus on traditions, festivals, and daily life.
- **Foodie**: Share insights into Senegalese cuisine, like your experience tasting *thiakry* or *bissap.*
- **Adventurer**: Highlight activities like kayaking in the Sine-Saloum Delta or trekking near the Senegal River.

2. Platforms for Sharing

1. Blogging

- **Best For**: In-depth storytelling and detailed travel guides.
- **How to Start**: Use platforms like WordPress or Medium. Create a visually appealing blog with large-format photos and easy navigation.
- **Content Ideas**:
    - "A Week in Senegal: From Dakar to the Delta"
    - "Top 10 Hidden Gems of Senegal for Cultural Travelers"

2. Social Media

Instagram

- **Best For**: Visual storytelling through high-quality images.
- **Tips for Engagement**:
    - Post carousel images to narrate a day in Senegal.
    - Use reels to showcase dynamic moments like drumming performances or bustling markets.
    - Include local hashtags like #DiscoverSenegal or #VisitSenegal.

Facebook

- **Best For**: Longer captions and community interaction.
- **How to Use**: Share photo albums with captions or create a group to document your travel adventures.

TikTok

- **Best For**: Short, creative videos.
- **Ideas**:
    - A time-lapse of sunset over the Sahel.
    - Step-by-step local recipes you learned, like preparing *ceebu jën*.

3. Travel Forums and Communities

- Share practical advice and recommendations on platforms like Lonely Planet's Thorntree or Reddit's r/travel.
- Post links to your detailed content for fellow travelers planning trips to Senegal.

4. Publishing Platforms

If you're an avid writer or photographer:

- Pitch stories to travel magazines like *National Geographic Traveler* or *Conde Nast Traveler*.
- Publish photo essays on platforms like Exposure.

3. Creating Engaging Content

Photos

- **Storytelling Through Images**:
    - Pair photos with short captions to contextualize the moment.

- Example: A photo of a fisherman at Lac Rose with the caption, "A salt harvester at sunrise, working in harmony with nature."
- **Editing Tips**:
  - Adjust saturation to enhance Senegal's vivid colors.
  - Use cropping to focus on specific details, like intricate patterns of local textiles.

Videos

- **Dynamic Storytelling**:
  - Create a video diary of your trip, mixing clips of bustling streets, serene landscapes, and local interactions.
  - Use narration or subtitles to guide viewers through your journey.
- **Cinematic Ideas**:
  - Drone footage of the Sine-Saloum Delta's waterways.
  - Slow-motion captures of traditional dances or wildlife movements.

Writing

- **Descriptive Language**: Bring your experiences to life. Instead of "The market was busy," try "The Sandaga Market pulsed with energy, its aisles overflowing with vibrant fabrics and the aroma of freshly fried *beignets*."
- **Quotes and Dialogues**: Incorporate conversations with locals for authenticity.
  - Example: A fisherman in Casamance sharing, "The river is our lifeline; it feeds us, guides us, and tells our stories."

4. Connecting with Your Audience

Engage Through Questions

Encourage interaction by asking for feedback or similar experiences.

- "Have you tried *bissap* before? What did you think?"
- "Which of these photos of Dakar's skyline is your favorite?"

Share Practical Tips

Help others plan their trips by offering actionable advice:

- Highlight the best time to visit Lac Rose for photography.
- Provide a packing list for rural adventures in the Sahel or Casamance.

Be Authentic

Focus on genuine experiences and avoid overly curated or staged content. Highlight challenges and surprises, such as navigating Senegal's roads or learning local phrases.

5. Preserving Your Memories

Scrapbooks and Prints

- Compile photos, ticket stubs, and pressed flowers into a physical scrapbook.
- Create a photo book through services like Shutterfly for a professional look.

Virtual Travel Journals

Use apps like Journi or Day One to document daily experiences with text, photos, and maps.

-

TRAVEL REFLECTIONS

Printed in Dunstable, United Kingdom

70012630R00165